SO-AZL-084

Holy Infant Jesus

Holy Infant Jesus

STORIES, DEVOTIONS, AND
PICTURES OF THE HOLY CHILD
AROUND THE WORLD

Ann Ball
and
Damian Hinojosa

A Crossroad Book
The Crossroad Publishing Company
New York

The Crossroad Publishing Company
481 Eighth Avenue, New York, NY 10001

© 2006 Ann Ball

All rights reserved. No part of this book may be reproduced, stored in a retrieval system, or transmitted, in any form or by any means, electronic, mechanical, photocopying, recording, or otherwise, without the written permission of The Crossroad Publishing Company.

This book is set in 11/14 AGaramond.

Printed in the United States of America

Library of Congress Cataloging-in-Publication Data

Ball, Ann.
   Holy infant Jesus : stories, devotions, and pictures of the Holy Child around the world / Ann Ball and Damian Hinojosa.
       p. cm.
   Includes bibliographical references and index.
   ISBN 0-8245-2407-1 (alk. paper)
   1. Holy Childhood, Devotion to. I. Hinojosa, Damian. II. Title.
   BX2159.C4B35 2006
   232.92'7—dc22
                                                      2006006249

1   2   3   4   5   6   7   8   9   10   10   09   08   07   06

Contents

1

Introduction

In the great mystery of the Incarnation, God the Son assumed human nature, thus becoming a historical person who lived from infancy to death. All that we know of the historical Jesus is recorded in the Gospels and some apocryphal literature. The evangelists St. Matthew and St. Luke give the infancy narrative of the birth of the Christ, the flight into Egypt, and the finding in the temple, but most of the childhood of Our Lord remains unknown. There is virtually nothing told of his day-to-day life before his public ministry. Some apocryphal literature attempted to fill in the gaps of these early years, but we have no surety of the truth of any of these stories. It is reasonable to suppose that the Holy Family lived a common life similar to other families of Galilee at the time. Extensive research by archaeologists of our own time has given us a picture of the day-to-day activities of people of their social status in the first century. And yet, even with the lack of factual, historical data, there is a great traditional devotion to Our Lord as a child.

We are familiar with the images of the Child Jesus in the manger scenes at Christmas, but throughout the world there is also a strong devotion to the Incarnate Word as a child. Devotion to his infancy has existed since the early years of Christianity. From the late Middle Ages to today, the Divine Child has been represented in visual images, each with its own particular history and popular religiosity.

Major saints and doctors of the church have outlined their devotion to the Child Jesus. Religious congregations are dedicated

1

in his name; he is artistically represented in European and New World drama, poetry, and painting. Apparitions of the Christ Child, alone and with the Virgin Mary, indicate his desire for this devotion. In the popular images of the Christ Child throughout the world, we can come to a deeper appreciation of this love for the Incarnate Word. They represent the "twin jewels" manifested in both the cultural diversity and universal sameness of the Catholic faith.

Childhood contains a promise of growth. Like the Wise Men who followed a star to find him, we can grow in love and understanding of the God Incarnate by meditating and reflecting on the Holy Child Jesus.

Clay Infant in manger—Little Sisters of Jesus
(see pp. 112-114)

II

The Child in Our Heart

The Meaning of the Devotion

By Susan Anderson Kerr

To understand why Christians love the Holy Child, the first step is to think about who a child is. He is full of life; he grows; he will be different the next time you see him. In fact, to restate devotion to the Holy Child in a sentence, you could write, "I will change." A child is dynamic, evolving, and new. The path into devotion to the Holy Child is through our own childhoods and those children we know well. To understand this infant, we go to the New Testament, where we find the same development in the Gospels of St. Matthew and St. Luke, the two evangelists who tell the story of his birth.

The next step to comprehending this devotion is to remember the long tradition within the church to understand how images functioned in the life of faith. The early Church Fathers realized that in seeing sacred images, believers could see the truths of their faith.

Christians realized that sacred images could be, like scripture, a way to present truth to the eye. Thus began the tradition of icons, images that didn't vary because the truths they represented were also constant. In the later Middle Ages and early Renaissance, sacred images began to reflect the different emphasis of the theology of the Western church, and they became more earthly— gold skies became blue, folds of garments became less angular and more curved, flesh tones and facial expressions were less stylized and more nuanced.

This means that when we look at the history of the images of the Christ Child, we can trace the evolution of ways to know the Word made flesh. Artists began to create images of the Good Shepherd, then representations of the cross and the Blessed Mother appeared, and later the crucifix. The Holy Child appeared only after believers comprehended the significance of these images.

Think of the development of early Christian art as a tree; then the Holy Child is the fruit that the tree bears. Artists only presented the Holy Child as a solitary figure once the church had dwelled three or four centuries with the teachings of Christ and his passion.

The archetype of the baby is imprinted in our psyches, and we use this image on a natural level to signal new life. We spontaneously turn to the symbol of a baby to picture beginnings; each New Year's day, naked infants mark the change in the calendar year. The figure of the baby gives us a way to imagine innocence, sweetness, gentleness, playfulness, and hope, those qualities that mark our lives when we have died to sin.

In the Middle Ages, the church celebrated the feast of Candlemas with a procession that circled the church. When the people sought to enter, the priest met the candle-bearing procession at the church door with a figure of the Holy Child in his arms. Since Candlemas is a feast where the universality of the light of Christ was revealed, we see here the meaning of this Holy Child's coming to save all.

In the Candlemas liturgy, as in some of the miracle stories of the Holy Child, he travels to the sufferer in order to heal, to save, and to rescue. The second person of the Trinity journeys to us, into our humanity, coming as a pilgrim out of love for us.

Like many devotions, love of the Holy Child is often handed down within families and promoted by religious orders. Those who know the Child Jesus well take him with them when they travel and teach others about the life of faith. Devotion to the Holy Child has often accompanied the Franciscans, Dominicans, Carmelites, Jesuits, and other religious congregations as they brought the Good News of salvation to other cultures.

Around the globe, many are blessed by the festivals that celebrate his birth. While Christians may decry the commercialism and paganism of the season of Christmas, where Christmas goes so does the name of the Christ Child. He brings joy to those who welcome such an opportunity to play, to express love, to be touched by wonder.

The cult of the Holy Child has today spread throughout the world. How can we account for this remarkable phenomenon, and what are we to make of the abundance of images and customs associated with devotion to the Holy Child? A verse from a nineteenth-century British hymn offers a good beginning:

> For he is our childhood's pattern,
>   Day by day like us he grew;
> He was little, weak, and helpless,
>   Tears and smiles like us he knew;
> And he feels for all our sadness,
>   And he shares in all our gladness.

Love for the Holy Child throughout the Christian world pours forth in retablos, votive offerings, and acts of gratitude. Let one voice summarize this multitude of devotions: In 1996 in Mexico City, a young woman went to a clinic for eye surgery. An apparition of the Holy Child of Atocha when she was seventeen years old assured her that she would not experience pain and she would be healed, and so it happened, to the astonishment of her doctors. Later, to witness to her regained eyesight, she cross-stitched this poem as a gift for him:

No sólo es la luz que a mi Mirada has dado,
La que me ha regresado del mundo sus colores,
Es más de tu milagro, oh Santo Niño amado,
El resplandor que brilla de tanto amor colmado
Que da luz a mi alma y fe a los corazones

Not only have you given sight to my eyes,
You've restored the world's colors to me,
But more than your miracle, oh beloved Holy Child,
The splendor that shines from such overflowing love
Gives light to my soul and faith to hearts.

Perla Buendía Jasso 1999 *

Holy Child of Atocha with mother

*Perla Buendía Jasso in Juan Pereira Nieves, *Cartas al Santo Niño de Atocha* (Fresnillo, Zacatecas, 1999), 157–59.

Looking at the Holy Child teaches us who we are. Our spiritual childhood has an ethical effect on us; seeing the Holy Child we yearn for his freedom and simplicity. The Holy Child calls us to emulate him in a mature, permanent way, and to be at home in the presence of our Heavenly Father.

Holy Child of Atocha

III

Playing with Baby Jesus

The History of Devotion to the Christ Child

Since his birth, there have always been people devoted to the Infant King. From the earliest centuries, the representation of the birth at Bethlehem has the Christ Child as its center, and the use of an image to represent the Incarnate Word covers centuries. From earliest times, the Mother of Jesus has been depicted with her son in her arms. Yet at some point, the Infant Jesus, in artistic depictions, was separated both from his mother and the birth narratives, and images of the Christ Child, sometimes called "holy dolls," began to be venerated in popular religiosity.

Popular devotion to the Christ Child has developed in a number of distinct and different histories; the Infant King reigns today under a plethora of titles with varied images and lore throughout the world. We can search for the history through early writings of the church, through the history of the liturgy, through the fine and performing arts, through recorded lives of the saints, and through the histories of religious orders. At best, we have a picture we cannot bring into clear focus. Studying the extant images of past and present, both the two dimensional images of the East and the three dimensional images that developed in the West, we see the beauty of the cultural diversity of this devotion. Through the representations of the Child God, we can gain a greater appreciation for the relevance of the infancy of Our Lord to our own lives.

The celebration of Christ's nativity on December 25 was introduced as a special feast in Rome about the middle of the fourth century. In the last half of the same century, we find a depiction of the nativity painted as a wall decoration in the Christian catacombs of Rome. In A.D. 440, Pope Sixtus III erected a manger, a replica of the crib at Bethlehem. Nativity or miracle plays flourished by the tenth century. In the early thirteenth century, St. Francis of Assisi is generally given credit for staging the first live nativity scenes, although there is no proof that an image of the Christ Child was used. The earliest known artifact depicting Jesus as a child separate from his mother dates from around 1260 and is a small marble statue generally attributed to Nicola Pisano. The child is depicted standing, his right hand raised in blessing, with his swaddling clothes starting below his chest, falling over his elbows and down his sides. Several replicas of this image have survived, in a variety of materials, and provide evidence of the rapid spread of devotional practices concerning the Christ Child.

In the fourteenth century, a custom arose in Germany and Austria of rocking the Christ Child's image in a cradle. The priest would carry the cradle to the altar and rock it while the congregation sang and prayed. The service ended with the devotional kissing of the Christ Child at the altar rail. The custom was a substitute for the nativity plays, which had been banned by the church because of abuses. By the sixteenth century, cradle rocking was also banned from the churches, but it survived for a long time as a devotional practice in convents and private homes. A number of these cradles are still extant.

Over the late Middle Ages, devotion to the Infant Jesus began to enter the private sphere of popular religiosity. Numerous documents show that images of the Christ Child began to be found in the homes of the nobility and in convents.

By the time of the Renaissance, some of the images were sculpted by famous artists, and many of the statues of the Christ Child were produced in convents. For the nuns, the very act of modeling the holy Child became a form of devotion, and they tenderly cared for the images entrusted to them. One such center was at the Dominican convent of Lucca where the nuns carried on a tradition established by Sister Costanza Micheli (born 1530) of making small devotional images of the Christ Child.

Later, Venerable Sister Isabella Chiara Fornari (born 1697), superior of the Franciscan Poor Clare Sisters in Todi, Italy, sculpted life-size images of both the Infant Jesus and the Infant Mary in a process using wax, which made them very lifelike. Perhaps her most famous sculpture is that of the Maria Bambina, an image of the Virgin Mary as a child, which is venerated in the motherhouse of the Sisters of Charity in Milan, Italy. Although the art of wax sculpting is dying out, small replicas of the image are still made by one of the sisters.

Two distinct sets of apparitions of the Christ Child did much to increase the devotion in the seventeenth century. Venerable Margaret Parigot (Margaret of the Blessed Sacrament of Beaune) (born 1619) was a humble cloistered Carmelite nun who was favored with a number of apparitions of the Christ Child. In one of these, he requested her to promote and spread the devotion to the Holy Infancy. She was assisted in this task by two friends— Father Olier of St. Sulpice and the Baron de Renty. John Jacob Olier (born 1608) founded the seminary of St. Sulpice, from which priests went out, spreading the devotion to the Holy Child throughout France. A pious layman, the Baron Gaston Jean Baptiste de Renty (born 1611) used his wealth to help publicize the devotion. He built a chapel to the Divine Infant, and Sister Margaret was later buried there. This chapel was destroyed during the French revolution.

In addition to Venerable Margaret, apparitions of the Christ Child to Father Cyril of the Mother of God Schokwilerg (died 1675), a discalced Carmelite in Prague, Czechoslovakia, strengthened devotion to the little Spanish image known as the Infant of

Prague. Father Cyril was a zealous promoter of devotion to this little image during his life, and the Carmelite order carried on his work after his death. The Infant of Prague is today possibly the best-known devotion to the Christ Child in the world.

A great many of the now famous images of the Holy Child date to the eighteenth and nineteenth centuries. This period saw a great increase in the devotion to the Holy Child. Known by various titles, the devotion spread throughout the world along with the growth and dissemination of religious orders, in particular the Jesuits, the Carmelites, the Theatines, and the Piarists. The images at this time present the Holy Child in new postures; images portrayed the Christ Child standing in a pose of blessing, with a crown on his head and holding a globe. Statues showing him asleep with his head resting on a skull, depicted with the symbols of the passion, and other representations became increasingly popular.

Infant Jesus of Prague

Infant Jesus with cross

From the first, certain statues became famous for miracles and for other favors given to devotees. Each developed its own lore and specific popular devotional practices. As the image gained fame, replicas were made so the people could bring the devotion home with them. As the cult spread to and through the New World, even more diverse representations of the Christ Child began to appear.

Although the Holy Child has, in many cases, acquired the externals of the culture where his image is venerated, the devotion still represents a piety that emphasizes the values of tenderness, innocence, and purity. So too the Christ Child exemplifies the supreme paradox of the Incarnation: the God who became the weakest of humanity—a baby—to draw hearts to himself as king of the universe.

Holy Dolls: Then and Now

From the late Middle Ages when the cult of the Holy Child began to enter the sphere of popular religious practice, often the devotional images were treated in many ways just as little girls treat their dolls. With the increase in realistic portrayal, the chubby little "Jesulein" or "Bambino" seemed to be made for holding, caressing, and kissing. The statues were given elaborate cradles and wardrobes. Generally the possessions of women and children, the images embellished the family oratory or a prayer space in a convent cell. Documents exist to show that during this time period in Florence, Italy, a "holy doll" was a common part of the trousseau of a woman about to be married, and also part of the dowry of a young woman entering the convent. It was hoped that the use of these holy images would excite the soul of the viewer to show devotion to the person the simulacrum represented.

Through the use of sacred imagery, the figures of the Child Jesus can enable the faithful to see and feel the childhood and vulnerability of the man God.

In 1860, the Dominican Blessed Giovanni Dominici Banchini (1356–1420) wrote a text of instructions suggesting to young mothers that they surround their children with holy dolls of Christ and the saints that they might keep these good examples always in front of them.

Although today's images of the Christ Child are most often devotional images of popular piety, there are some who follow Dominici's suggestions and have created holy images made specifically for children to play with. Teri O'Toole is the designer for Soft Saints, a company with the avowed goal of creating positive role models through their collector dolls. The company produces dolls representing a number of Catholic saints and an image of the Christ Child that comes with its own crib. Teri sees her work

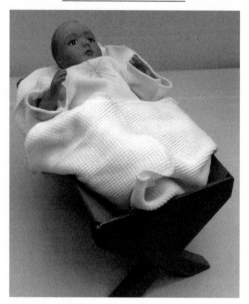

Soft Saints doll

as a mission and finds it interesting to watch the effect the dolls have on people, especially on the elderly, who seem to feel as if they are really taking care of the Infant Jesus when they hold that particular doll. Sandra Maola, one of the cofounders of Faith-filled Friends, says that she and her partner, Anna Pallisco, began to develop toys that promote the lives of biblical characters and saints of the church to counteract the message that some secular dolls were sending to young children. They were inspired to make faith-based dolls that inspire children and reinforce positive and character-building virtues. Their dolls give children the visual tools and hands-on images they need as a means of learning.

A tiny pocket doll depicting the Infant Jesus was created by Billie Walter, a Third Order Carmelite. Small enough to hold in the palm of the hand, the doll was made to help teach children to talk to Jesus. It can encourage them to pray as they play. Several hundred of the puff dolls have traveled around the world: to Russia, to an orphanage in Yugoslavia, via a missionary in India, and

*Faith-filled
Friend
Jesus doll*

*Infant Jesus pocket
dolls by Billie Walter*

to a home for abused children as well as a women's prison in California. Billie first thought of the pocket baby Jesus doll when she noticed the fear in the eyes of the children in the child abuse section of the county government office where she worked. She made some of the simple little dolls and gave them to the chaplain to distribute. Being able to hold the Child Jesus in their hand seemed to bring a little peace to these children. Later, more of the dolls were made by some former prisoners.

From the time devotion to the Infant Jesus separated from the Christmas celebrations and entered the sphere of popular religious practice, the child has been celebrated in literature and art. The expression of devotion to the Child Jesus became as diverse in its representations as human imagination.

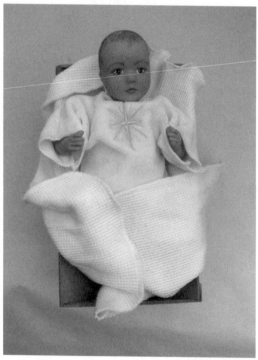

Soft Saints doll

IV

Come Let Us Adore Him

Old World Traditions

From the twelfth to the sixteenth centuries popular Christian celebrations of the nativity flourished, not only in churches and monasteries, but in homes as well. Artists and musicians and poets depict God's grace in the lives of angels, kings, shepherds, and even through animals. The oldest extant Christmas legend is recounted by Gregory of Tours in his collection of miracle stories from the year 594. Other popular legends were also in circulation: at the midnight hour cattle could speak, bees awoke and buzzed, and birds produced the sweetest song, which could be heard only by the faithful.

Medieval Liturgical Drama

The earliest medieval plays focused on the journey of the Three Kings. These plays show that they followed a star desiring to pay homage to a newborn king as prophecy foretold. One of the oldest plays about the Three Kings, written in the year 1200, is titled *El Auto de los Reyes Magos.* The first scene begins with a discussion among the Three Kings, who are named Gaspar, Melchior, and Balthasar and who reveal to the audience the meaning of the glorious star in the sky. In scene two they follow the star in search of the newborn king. Even though the kings do not know much about the Infant Jesus, in the third scene King Herod questions them while on their journey. The Wise Men know that the new-born king will take care of all those who adore him just like any earthly king. The Three Kings illustrate to the audience that the reign of the Infant King concerns a kingdom that includes every-one who honors and adores the newborn king. After seeing the Christ Child, they do not fear Herod's threats and take an alter-nate route home. As the play concludes, a confused Herod ques-tions the rabbis about the truth of the newborn king, and at last one rabbi proclaims that indeed prophecy has been fulfilled.

Other short and simple anonymous plays about the Christ Child allowed the audience to witness through drama how God's infinite love came down from heaven. In addition, the journey of the Three Kings to the birthplace of the baby Jesus inspired the audience to give homage of the newborn king during their own pilgrimage on earth. The plays written about the birth of Jesus indicate that there probably existed a developed liturgical drama, a collection of popular Christmas poems, and other artistic repre-sentations of the Christ Child in the Middle Ages.

A Renaissance play entitled *The Representation of the Birth of Our Lord* by Jorge Manrique two hundred years later concludes with allegorical figures like the cross, nails, a whip, and wounds following the appearance of angels and saints, all gathering in the concluding scene as they dance around and honor the Child Jesus. Even though presented as a child, the audience is reminded that evil will have an effect on the baby who will one day suffer for all.

Artists and the Child Jesus

Both paintings and statues still existing from the Middle Ages illustrate that Christ's kingdom extends the title of queen to his mother, often portrayed with a crown or halo. Artists continued to present the Christ Child in a traditional way in his mother's arms, while popular Christmas songs and plays that placed the baby in a manger adored by his mother at a distance began to change the way in which the image of the mother and child was portrayed.

Some artists became well known for their artistic style, especially for presenting the theme of mother and child. Some of the artists began to sign their paintings, especially those who focused on presenting the Christ Child in a personalized way. One of these earlier known artists is Giotto (1266–1336), who painted several frescos in which the Christ Child becomes the most prominent figure in the work of art even though he is the smallest person in the work. Some of these include *The First Christmas at Greccio* (c. 1297–1300) and *The Flight into Egypt* (c. 1304–1306). His two panels *Madonna Enthroned* (1310) and *Madonna and Child* (c. 1320–1330) present the child in different and unique perspectives, in the clothing and in the positioning of Jesus' hands into different gestures.

In his painting of the Virgin and Child, Beato Fra Angelico (1387–1455) presents the Christ Child standing upright in her lap imparting a blessing with his right hand while holding an orbis in his left hand. His mother's left hand supports his balance since he has not yet learned to walk. The artist uses a miniature version of an adult's body for this figure of the Christ Child, which is wearing a deep red sleeveless tunic. Fra Angelico illustrates the divinity of the child by painting around his head a golden aureola containing three of the four points of a red cross. This image presents the Christ Child already undertaking his mission on earth as understood in Greek iconography.

As the Christ Child became the foremost figure in the mother and child arrangement artists began to present the Child Jesus in a more human way, breaking from the traditional artistic perspective. The gifted artist Raphael (1483–1520) painted his *Madonna and Child with Young Saint John* (1507) in homage to both Gospel figures as children. The Virgin Mary seated between the two children cares for them both as she reads from a book. She supports the child John with her right hand while upholding the Christ Child, who leans on her right knee. Wearing only a simple white sash around his waist and nothing else, Jesus reaches out to touch the small bird that John holds in his hands. John, who is taller and has more hair, wears a tunic made of fur held in place with a cord. The meeting between the two infants has no reference in the New Testament; however, it seems important to note that in these representations of holy children, the artistic creation signifies to some degree the devotion given to Christ and St. John in their infant stage of life. Here Raphael clearly illustrates to the viewer that the innocence of these two children becomes an important dimension of their lives when later undertaking their mission as men.

Another artist, Bronzino (1503–1572), presented his image of the Christ Child with John the Baptist as a child in a unique context. While St. Joseph and Mary recline to watch over the two

*Detail of painting by
Fra Angelico*

Madonna of the Magnificat
by Sandro Boticelli

children, John is depicted embracing Jesus, who lies in front of him asleep on top of a regal blue pillow. The Christ Child in an extended position sleeps partly wrapped in swaddling clothes while only John's small head and right side are visible.

Sandro Botticelli (1445–1510) brings to light the aspect of adoring the Child Jesus. In his *Madonna of the Magnificat* (c. 1483–1485), the Child Jesus balanced on his mother's lap is only partly covered with a white cloth, exposing his entire torso, both arms, and his right leg. Botticelli adorns all the other figures in colorful clothing only exposing their faces, necks, and hands. This contrast is further developed by the artist who paints the Child Jesus glancing into the space above while the Madonna and all others glance downward toward the written Word of God, illustrating the harmony between the human and the divine. In his painting *Adoration* (c. 1482–1485), Botticelli again positioned most of the figures in adoration staring in the direction of the mother and child while others glance toward the heavens. The child's mother, Mary, supports his right arm as it extends to touch the page of the New Testament where the Magnificat is clearly inscribed, signaling here the importance of the Word made flesh. The child's left hand, which is held in his mother's left hand, grasps a half-peeled pomegranate, symbolizing the resurrection.

In Michaelangelo's *Holy Family with the Infant St. John the Baptist* (c. 1503) the Mother of Christ sitting on the ground turns to glance upward behind her right shoulder as she passes the Infant Jesus to St. Joseph, who sits behind her. The artist presents an old Joseph and a young Mary, both dressed in flowing material of bright colors while the Infant Jesus is presented without any clothing, suggesting the natural innocence of the Christ Child. In the distant right portion of the circular painting glares the infant John the Baptist clothed in a fur tunic bearing a simple shepherd's staff in his left hand. All of the figures have the appearance of ordinary humans lacking a halo or any other symbols to indicate their sanctity.

The images of the infants Jesus and St. John in painting reached a superior level of expression in the two works of Leonardo da Vinci (1452–1519) entitled *Madonna of the Rocks*. The Franciscans in Milan commissioned Leonardo da Vinci to paint his first version of *Madonna of the Rocks* for their chapel in honor of the feast of the Immaculate Conception (c. 1493–1495). In this large retablo or panel for the chapel, da Vinci situates the Virgin Mary in the center of the work, placing the children on the ground within close proximity as she watches over them. The Infant Jesus, seated naked with his legs crossed, supports himself in an upright position with his left arm. With his right hand he imparts a blessing as he glances upward in a direction away from both his mother and St. John while the Virgin Mary extends her left hand in the direction of her son's head. A large angel dressed in colorful clothing sits behind the Infant Jesus supporting him

*Madonna of the Rocks
by Leonardo da Vinci*

with the left hand while pointing at the infant John with the right hand. With her right arm and blue garment extended over his shoulders the Virgin Mary uses her hand to support the infant John, who kneels at her side with his hands joined in prayer, wearing only a simple cloth around his torso. In the second version of the same painting (c. 1506–1508) the artist added halos to the three human figures and incorporated into the infant John's prayerful posture a tall thin cross resembling a shepherd's staff.

In the seventeenth century Peter Paul Rubens (1577–1640) painted the infants Jesus and St. John the Baptist alone playing in a idyllic setting without the protections of the Blessed Virgin Mary. The two children occupy the primary space of the painting along with a spotless white lamb whose head they gently caress. The infant John, standing partially clad with animal fur, gently touches the lamb with both hands as he meaningfully stares at the face of the Infant Jesus. The Child Jesus, seated without clothing on a rock covered with a red cloth, supports his weight with his left hand while placing his right hand on the lamb's head. Rubens metaphorically presents the themes of innocence and purity indicated by the visages and loving gestures of the two children, without incorporating halos, regal clothing, scepters, or even a cross or shepherd's staff to indicate the sanctity of these two innocent biblical figures. The implicit moral lesson is that even a simple gesture of kindness demonstrates the greatest virtue of love.

While these are only some of the works of great artists of the Old World, there are many others whose artistic legacies have led people in the present age to reflect upon and to recognize the important devotions that still remain significant in the spiritual lives of ordinary people today. The reproduction of artistic images and paintings of the past centuries has also provided testimony of the faithful whose love of God found itself creatively manifested, not only in the presence of a mother holding her child, but also in the mere presence of innocent children themselves.

Old World Poetry and the Christ Child

Written in the eleventh century, one of the earliest popular poems about the Infant Jesus is from Spain and is called a "villancico." Entitled "A Song to Quiet the Child, Hush My Little Child," the short lyric poem was composed by a nun for her sisters in the convent and recalls that the Holy and Divine Child cried just like other babies. To relieve the pains he suffers as a child, the poet offers words of consolation to the Infant Jesus telling him in these two stanzas that his suffering will not last long as they also call on the angels to console him.

> Calladvos, Señor, / nuestro Redentor,
> que vuestro dolor, / durará poquito.
> > Angeles del cielo, / venid dar Consuelo
> > A este mozuelo / Jesús tan bonito.

Quiet, O Lord, our Redeemer
Your pain will last only a while.
> Angels of heaven, come and give solace
> To this cute little one, Jesus so pretty.

These two stanzas recall that the Lord "our Redeemer" despite his innocence and charming disposition will know pain and endure human suffering in his life.

Miracle stories written in poetic form were composed in great part by learned clerics who wrote and translated miracle stories into the various languages used at the time. While most miracle stories reveal the miracles of Our Lady the Mother of Jesus, a few poems focus specifically on the Christ Child. One such poem, found in the Book of the Three Kings of the Orient, tells how the Holy Family fled to Egypt to protect the baby Jesus from Herod's order to kill all infant males. A family who offers them refuge in Egypt is blessed with the miracle of the healing of their own new-born baby. Their son is miraculously cured of leprosy after the Virgin Mary, called the "Gloriosa," bathes their son in the same tub of water she has used for the Infant Jesus. The mother of the cured child attributes the miracle to the presence of the Virgin Mary's child, who she proclaims is God.

The mystic and doctor of the church St. Teresa of Avila, three hundred years later, also uses the dynamic of the Three Kings in expressing her devotion to the Christ Child.

Con los Reyes

Pues que la estrella
Es ya llegada
Va con los Reyes
La mi manada
Vamos todos juntos
A ver al Mesías

Que vemos cumplidas
Todas las profecías
Pues en nuestros días
Nos es ya llegada,
Van con los Reyes
La mi manada.

Now that the star
Has already arrived,
Go with the Kings
My dear little flock.
We are going together
To see the Messiah
Since we see fulfilled
All the prophecies
Now that in our day
He as already arrived,
They are going with the Kings
My dear little flock.

In this stanza and refrain, we see again the invitation to join the kings following the star in search of the Child Jesus whose birth was foretold in the prophecies of long ago. The shepherds with their flocks also seek to adore him and to pay him homage. In this poem St. Teresa of Avila focuses on the popular celebration of the Divine Child's epiphany and included the reenactment of the search for the newborn king until all arrive in Bethlehem.

New World Traditions

The missionaries established in America Christmas customs that they brought from the different parts of their homeland. In the context of the nativity scene already popular at this time, the audience or reader sees that Jesus' mother wraps the infant in swaddling clothes and places him in a manger so that the world may share her joy. Lying in a manger before his parents, Jesus provides them with the experience of responding to his love in an unconditional way. The presence of Joseph and Mary reminds us that God's infinite love is bestowed from heaven upon all who come to adore the Christ Child on earth.

In the New World poets created new expressions about traditional devotions to the Christ Child. One of the most significant among these poets was Sor Juana Inés de la Cruz, a brilliant nun whose writings also include illustrious *villancicos* about the baby Jesus. As a sister in the Convent of San Jerónimo in Mexico City, she spent her life perfecting her own poetic expression. One example of her highly stylized poetry presents the Christ Child in relation to the elements of earth, wind, fire, and water.

Primero Nocturno, 283, Villancico I, (Navidad 1689)

Por celebrar del Infante
El temporal Nacimiento,
Los cuatro elementos vienen:
Agua, Tierra, y Aire y Fuego.

Con razón, pues se compone
La humanidad de su Cuerpo
De Agua, Fuego, Tierra y Aire,
Limpia, puro, frágil, fresco.

En el Infante mejoran
Sus Calidades y centros,
Pues les dan mejor esfera
Ojos, Pecho, Carne, Aliento.

A tanto favor rendidos,
En amorosos obsequios
Buscan, sirven quieren, aman,
Prestos, finos, puros, tiernos. (p. 260)

By celebrating the Infant
His earthly birth on earth,
The four elements come together
Water, Earth, and Air and Fire.

Well and with reason comes to be
The Human nature of his body
Of Water, Fire, Earth and Air
Clean, pure, fragile, fresh.

In the Infant do improve
His qualities and centers (senses),
Since they provide a better sphere
Eyes, Bosom, Flesh, Breath.

For so much favor, given over
In loving offering,
They search, they serve, they desire, they love
So ready, so fine, so pure, so delicate.

In her poetic description of the Christ Child's attributes, Sor Juana associates respectively the four elements of water, fire, earth, and air with four physical aspects or spheres of the infant Jesus: eyes, bosom, flesh, breath. She also associates these elements of his human nature collectively with some spiritual attributes: to search, to serve, to desire, and to love.

The plays and poems of the Old and New Worlds illustrate how wise and gifted people would inspire others to admire, to honor, and to adore the Christ Child in their day. As a protagonist in literature and drama, the Infant Jesus reveals the love of

God in such a way that those who come to worship him do not see him as an awe-inspiring judge or as a strict model to imitate but rather as a human person whose innocent presence serves as the basis of his being, even in later years when he began to encounter the effects of sinful people in the world.

These among others are not new lessons for the medieval and Renaissance audiences of Europe. People understood that Christ the King also inspires a unique response from each person in his kingdom. St. Joseph and the Virgin Mary in the nativity scene demonstrate unique aspects in responding to God's call. In the case of the Three Kings, their vocation was to spread the Good News about the fulfillment of prophecy: they responded by following the star that would guide them to the newborn king. Today their presence in the nativity scene continues to invite others to follow their hearts and to come to adore the Christ Child, who is the newborn king.

V

They Believed and They Saw

Visions of the Child Jesus

Among the phenomenal experiences in the history of Christian spirituality, a number of people have had visions of the Infant Jesus. Religious women in convents, people in palaces, and ordinary people with extraordinary faith in Jesus Christ have seen visions of the Christ Child or have heard his voice calling. The earliest recorded experience occurred with Pope Alexander I (A.D. 118) who had a vision of Jesus as an infant. Most individuals who have written down their visions of the Child Jesus have also received recognition as a venerable, blessed, or canonized person in the Catholic Church.

Visions help to understand why the Christ Child wanted to communicate at such an early age. Some important criteria for understanding a vision are the spirituality of the visionary as well as the coherency of the message expressed and, therefore, any spiritual consequences. Unlike apparitions, visions do not include any material manifestation of the divine presence.

The visionary often remains quiet about this religious experience and is unlikely to publish any story.

In the Middle Ages, churches, convents, and monasteries began to record and document visions of the Christ Child. During the early years of the Franciscan Order, both St. Francis of Assisi and St. Clare received visions of the Infant Jesus. This did not seem like a surprise for St. Francis, who also reported that the Cross of San Damiano spoke to him. The spiritual success of the

Franciscan nativity scene in modern times indicates the providential history of these devotional figures of the Holy Family, the shepherds, and the Three Kings throughout the centuries.

During the Counter-Reformation a number of holy men and women record in their spiritual diaries the experiences of seeing Christ as a small child who appears unexpectedly. Sr. Bernardine Realino (1530–1616) sees the Infant Jesus and recognizes this religious experience as a blessing among many others he received in his life.

Visions and Representations

In the artistic reproduction of Christian images, some holy men and women have been depicted holding the Child Jesus as if it were an adaptation of the traditional image of the mother and child. Some artists created images of saints in the presence of or even holding the Christ Child, like the image of St. Joseph holding his Son. The images of other saints with the Christ Child

St. Francis of Assisi

St. Clare

*Ven. Clara Fey with
the Christ Child*

*St. Rose of Lima
with the Chirst Child*

St. Cajetan

*St. Anthony with
the Christ Child*

introduced into popular devotion another aspect of the Christ Child: the Infant Jesus visits his devotees. The artistic representations of saints depicted with the Christ Child indicate that these saints have witnessed visions of the Infant Jesus. These include St. Anthony of Padua (1195–1231), St. Cajetan (1480–1547), founder of the Theatines, and the Third Order Dominican St. Rose of Lima (1586–1617).

In Italy, St. Vincent Pallotti (1795–1850) founded the Society of the Catholic Apostolate or the Pallotines. During his life as a priest he had a vision of the Christ Child that inspired him to commission a statue of the Holy Bambino. He hoped that this would inspire others to witness the innocence of the Christ Child represented by the lifelike figure. On certain occasions, as in the case of St. Vincent, the Christ Child is too young to speak and expresses his love simply by reaching out to all as he lies in the manger.

Venerable Clara Fey, who lived in Aachen, saw the Infant Jesus dressed as a poor little boy. While walking through town the Christ Child appeared to her in 1826. She did not recognize who he was and asked him where he lived. He replied that he was the poor Child Jesus and that he had many poor little brothers and sisters. She then saw the presence of the Infant Jesus in the faces of the destitute children in the street. The manifestation of Christ's presence in the faces of the poor children inspired her to establish a new religious order, the Sisters of the Poor Child Jesus, who continue to care for underprivileged children.

Cornelia Connelly founded a religious order called the Society of the Holy Child Jesus. She lived in England (1809–1879) as a convert to Catholicism and saw how the virtues of poverty, suffering, and obedience had deeper meaning in the presence of the Jesus born in a stable. The rule of her order promoted devotion to the Christ Child by professing a life of simplicity and humility as

Venerable Cornelia Connelly

experienced by Jesus and his mother, Mary, on the solemn occasion of his birth. Cornelia taught her religious sisters that the Incarnate Word as seen in the Child Jesus exemplifies the way in which devotion requires a total response to the Spirit. She painted a portrait of the Holy Child Jesus to promote devotion to the Christ Child.

Spiritual Legacies and Devotion
to the Christ Child

The spiritual tradition of the Spanish Carmelite Teresa of Jesus (1515–1582), doctor of the church, continued as other sisters and priests embraced a devotion to the Christ Child. In 1637, Fr.

Holy Child painted by Cornelia Connelly

Cyril of the Holy Mother of God, a Carmelite priest, heard the voice of the Infant of Prague, who instructed him to repair the original statue brought to their convent from Spain, "Give Me My hands and I will give you peace. The more you honor me, the more I will bless you." In response to one of the priest's particular requests, the Christ Child told him to place the Infant of Prague statue near the sacristy. Badly needed assistance for church repairs soon arrived. Carmelite Sister Margaret of Beaune, inspired by a vision of the Christ Child in 1836, promoted devotion to the Infant Jesus at the popular level and, later in history, the Carmelite St. Thérèse of Lisieux embraced the spirituality of the Infant Child, inspiring many others to do the same.

Visions of the Christ Child
in the Twentieth Century

Sister Lucia dos Santos
Visionary of Fatima, Portugal

Many of those who have received visions of the Blessed Virgin Mary have also witnessed both mother and child appearing on Christmas Day or Christmas Eve. Sr. Lucia dos Santos (1907–2005), who witnessed the apparitions of the Virgin Mary at Fatima, also records that she received a vision of both mother and child in the month of December.

Sister Josefa Menendez
Society of the Sacred Heart of Jesus, Spain

Sr. Josefa Menendez, a member of the Society of the Sacred Heart of Jesus (1890–1923), wrote that she saw "Our Lady" with the

In addition to seeing Our Lady of Fatima,
Lucio dos Santos (middle) also saw the Child Jesus

*Sister Josefa Menendez
had visions of the Christ Child*

Christ Child before and after receiving Communion at Midnight Mass, December 24, 1920. Once seated in her place, she interpreted his grasping reach as an invitation to offer her hand. She gave explicit details of this experience with the newborn child, unable to speak, who clutched her finger as a gesture of love. Josefa describes as well the "delicious aroma" in the area surrounding them. The Virgin Mary invited her to kiss the feet of God and then told her, "He is all love." During this vision Josefa commented on the unique quality of the Holy Child's clothing. The material, something she had never seen before, seemed as light as foam and did not detract from the aura surrounding the Christ Child's head.

In her description of another vision, the Christ Child affirms that he hears all appeals because he is always near. This helps us to understand how the Infant Jesus communicates. First, Josefa hears Christ Child's voice calling. The voice many times remains unheard; only those who listen with the soul can hear and call back to the Christ Child. Josefa writes that her soul became more and more "attuned to the littleness of the Infant God."

Josefa learns that the Infant Jesus delivers his message to the soul of each person, not to the mind or to the individual's ability to reason. On December 25, 1922, Josefa saw the Christ Child, who appeared quite tiny, wrapped in a white veil. Only his little hands and feet remained visible and his hair was quite short. She describes his voice several times as the tenderest and sweetest voice as he proclaimed himself King. The Infant Jesus requested of Josefa a tunic—not a material one but rather a spiritual tunic made of souls. He had asked her to bring more souls to him so that they might adore him as well, saying that his heart loved the souls of those who adored him. As Sr. Josefa describes the experience, her writings illustrate that it is the human spirit or soul that hears the voice of the Christ Child.

Josefa describes the physical nature of the Infant Jesus with few details emphasizing that he seemed all aglow in his appearances. She admits her inability to describe his remarkable beauty noting that the "tender sweetness of his voice was ineffable." His tiny disposition serves in attracting others to love him and also as a way of measuring humility in serving him. The Infant Jesus informed Josefa that he wanted her to become even smaller than he, not physically smaller, but spiritually smaller through simplicity, humility, and promptness in obedience.

In a subsequent vision, the Virgin Mary appeared with the Christ Child in her arms, wrapped in a white veil. While she could not see him, she recalls again hearing his sweet voice speak of his request for a little tunic adorned with many souls. He encourages her to see that those who respond to his expectations bring the greatest consolation to his heart. The Virgin Mary explained on this occasion that the ungrateful heart leads a person to think of himself more than necessary while a heart full of love for her son Jesus allows someone to become as spiritually small as the heart of the Christ Child. The lesson implied here is a reminder that the smaller the person spiritually, the more room there is for others in the heart.

Sister María Angélica Alvarez Icaza, VSM
Visitation Sisters, Mexico

Sister María Angélica, a Visitation Sister (1887–1977), wrote extensively about her spiritual experiences, including her visions of the Child Jesus, in her writings entitled "Encantos del Amor Divino." A native of Mexico, she lived in Spain from 1916 to 1948 and returned to Mexico as the foundress and superior of the new community. In this way she restored the Order of the Visitation in Mexico after the Catholic Church ceased to suffer persecution.

In one description of a vision of the Christ Child she wrote that she considered the phenomenon of these visions as "gracia regalada" or God's grace given as a gift. She also wrote that the nature of Christ's infancy manifests itself powerfully in the mystery of the Incarnate Word and is the most perfect example of God in a weak, loving, and tender state. God present as the Christ Child communicates innocence and love without words.

The Divine Child presented himself suddenly in her little room, which has a window. Without a table, she wrote on the floor, and here is where the Christ Child appeared, but she continued to write until pausing to tell him as if speaking to any little child, "Don't take away my time since I have a lot to do." Regardless, she still felt his burning love in her heart. Sr. María Angélica wrote that she did not pursue or request this vision, but rather Jesus united himself to her in prayer and told her, "I am your *dueño*" or master (November 1914).

In describing a subsequent vision, Sr. María Angélica explains the context in which the visions manifested themselves. She writes that, as in a game or amusement, great illuminations about Christian mysteries reveal themselves to her in her soul. Consistent with other reports about visions, the Child Jesus appeals to and communicates with the soul of his followers and not with their intellect. She recalls that one day while ringing the bell for a community event the Child Jesus appeared to her. He then quickly disappeared after spending a few moments in joyful play with the bell as she rang it. Following this, she recorded two specific details about the nature of her visions. The moment of the vision's revelation always caught her off guard while distracted or when her mind was occupied in imaginative thought. The other detail explains that she sees the attributes of an omnipotent and eternal God in her vision of the Christ Child or something new about the ineffable mystery of the Holy Trinity or some other lofty intellectual subject.

Sister María Angélica described some of her religious experiences in poetry. One of the more detailed descriptions of her vision of the Christ Child imitates the simplicity of century-old *villancicos*.

Seventh Account of the Conscience, No. 167
Se Relata una aparición del Niño Jesús

Era el Niño encantador
Que en su ternura exquisite,
Para probarme su amor,
Varias veces me visita.

De su rostro que extasía
A los angeles del cielo,
Una viva luz partía
Que me daba gran Consuelo.

Ya se sabe, de repente,
El amor hablar no pudo
Que es a veces elocuente
Y en ocasiones es mudo.

El trabajo silencioso
Continuábamos los dos;
Y en verdad el Niño hermoso
Trabajaba como Dios . . .

Por fin la tarea concluimos
Y con ternura infinita
Por el convento nos fuimos
A poner agua bendita.

¡Oh quién el retrato hiciera,
De este Niño encantador!
¡Quién bosquejarnos pudiera
Su belleza y esplendor!

¡Con qué pincel, ni pintura,
Se pudiera retratar
Su delicada figura
Inconcebible y sin par! (June 1915)

An Account of an Apparition of the Child Jesus

He was an enchanting Child
Who in his exquisite tenderness (gentleness),
To show his love for me
Visits me from time to time.

From his face, ecstasy
To the angels in heaven,

A vivid light shone forth
Which gave me great consolation.

Already it is known that all of a sudden
Love (the Christ Child) could not speak
And at times he is eloquent
While on other occasions he is mute.

The work so quietly done
We continued, the two of us;
And in truth, the beautiful Child
Worked like God . . .

We eventually completed the task
And with infinite tenderness
Throughout the convent we went
Sprinkling holy water.

With regard to his ineffable appearance and the inability to
describe the Child Jesus as seen in her visions, the following stanzas express the limitations of the human condition while illustrating the qualities of the Infant Jesus, who enchants everyone in a
unique way.

Oh, who could ever create a portrait
Of this enchanting Child!
Oh, who could ever sketch for us
His beauty and his splendor!
With what pencil, not even with paint,
Could anyone be able to portray
His delicate figure
Inconceivable and without equal!

The writings of Sr. María Angélica concerning her visions of
the Child Jesus shed light on the devotion to Christ's infancy. This

spirituality is typical in comparison with the experiences of others who have been sanctified by a vision of the Christ Child. As written simply and clearly by this witness, the Child Jesus in his infant encounters, with total simplicity, converted the biggest into the smallest and the smallest into the greatest.

Mother Clara del Carmen Aguilera
The Franciscan Sisters of the Immaculate Conception, Mexico

A series of visions of the Child Jesus to Mother Clara del Carmen Aguilera (b. 1867) inspired a devotion to Jesus as Niño Fundador, or Founder of the Franciscan Sisters of the Immaculate Conception. In October 1894, Clara was at Mass at the church in Celaya, Guanajuato, praying to discern her vocation in life. During the consecration, she saw a ray of light descending and also a beautiful child, half dressed, floating on a cloud. The Christ Child held out his arms, raising up his palms. Gathering her courage, she told the beautiful child of her desire to be a religious sister and then asked him for counsel. When he confirmed that she should be a religious sister, she pointed out that her partial deafness and her poverty would be obstacles to her entrance into religious life. He told her that he would be her doctor and her medicine and that he would also provide for her vocation. When she mentioned the beautiful cloud on which he was standing, he told her the cloud represented her prayers.

The following month during Mass, she saw a beautiful child standing near the priest at Communion. He told her that there was a hidden place he wanted her to be, and that he would be there with her. He instructed her to tell her confessor of his words and to do as the priest instructed her.

A few days later she saw the Christ Child again after receiving Communion and, on the order of her confessor, she told him

*Niño Fundador as seen
by Mother Clara*

that she was to ask for a sign. The Christ Child stated that in proof of his promises she would be cured. The hearing in her right ear was fully restored, the ear in which she had first heard the Child Jesus' voice. And all came to pass as the child had said.

Young Clara went to Mexico City to visit the founders of the Franciscan Sisters of the Immaculate Conception, and she heard the voice of the Christ Child telling her that this was the place where he wanted her to minister. She joined the small congregation and professed her religious vows.

In an apparition at the end of 1903, the Holy Child told Mother Clara that she would lead the little congregation to accomplish big tasks. Despite the limitations of a small community, Mother Clara accepted with the understanding that the "Niño Jesús" would assist as the founder of all their spiritual endeavors. On October 22, 1904, the Child Jesus again appeared to Mother Clara, dressed and sitting on a cloud. When she asked why he was seated and dressed in that manner, he replied, "Because I am the Founder." He instructed her to make the first statue of the Niño Jesús Fundador, which is now venerated in their convent in Coyoacán, Mexico. Prayerful petitions to the little Founder resulted in numerous favors and graces, and devotion to Christ's infancy under this name began to grow and spread. The novena in his honor details nine miracles attributed to him between 1898 and 1942. These include five cures of serious health problems, three of persons on death row, and the return of a large sum of money to an impoverished family.

Niño Jesús Fundador de las Hermanas Franciscanas continues to show his predilection for the marginalized of society just as do the Franciscan Sisters of the Immaculate Conception who also minister in his name. Under this title, the community celebrates a feast in his honor each October 22. Copies of the original image are taken to each new foundation of a convent where the statue is venerated by the sisters as well as by the poor, sick, and abandoned whom they serve.

Concepción Cabrera de Armida
The Works of the Cross, Mexico

Venerable Concepción Cabrera de Armida (1862–1937), known most often simply as Conchita, is one of the most remarkable women of the church in the twentieth century. Not a saint of the cloister, she was a wife and the mother of nine children. A warm and loving woman who constantly displayed all the virtues proper to her state in life, she was also a great mystic. In her sixty-six volume spiritual diary, Conchita has left a record of an especially favored soul who received extraordinary graces.

Widowed at a young age, Conchita inspired five Works of the Cross, which include two religious orders: The Religious of the Cross of the Sacred Heart of Jesus, a contemplative congregation of nuns of perpetual adoration, and, with Father Felix Rougier, the Missionaries of the Holy Spirit, a congregation of priests whose special mission is the direction of souls.

In addition to numerous other visions, Conchita had a vision in which the Christ Child rested in her lap. In her description of this experience, she wrote that while seated on the floor, the Child Jesus, alive and well, appeared resting in her lap. He allowed her to touch his light-colored hair. He wore a purple tunic made of felt. From time to time he gazed at her; this filled her with a "divine sensation" that was impossible for her to describe.

Sister Faustina Kowalska
Poland

As recorded in her spiritual diaries, Sr. Faustina has received more visions of the Christ Child than any other saint (1905–1938). In the last four years of her life she kept a spiritual diary, her first entry recording the visions occurs in the spring of 1928. On this occasion the Virgin Mary holding the Infant Jesus in her arms appeared to Sr. Faustina. This experience does not occur again until six years later when the Virgin Mary again appears with her son in her arms. Sr. Faustina recorded that on this occasion the Christ Child spoke to her. The vision quickly vanished and, as written by other visionaries, the Divine Child's astonishing presence left a deep impression in her heart. Soon after this experience she received an inner locution while at prayer, directing her to meditate on the mystery of the Incarnation.

Sr. Faustina's writings confirm the messages recorded by other visionaries and, in general, promote the notion of purity of heart and purity of intention. She writes that true devotion does not promote complacency through following a schedule of prayer alone. She states that each devotion should assist a person to strive for a life of recollection, which in turn allows the soul to hear the sweet voice of the Christ Child. As said to other visionaries, the Infant Jesus revealed to Sr. Faustina that the fervent ardor of her

*The mystic
and mother Conchita*

*Saint Faustina often saw
the Christ Child*

own heart pleased him immensely (1936). The Child Jesus also confirmed that he could not act on just any soul—only on the souls of those who had faith alive in their hearts.

Reflecting on the nature of the kingdom of God on earth, the Infant Jesus came again and spoke to her in a lengthy conversation (June 1938). The Christ Child stated that his kingdom on earth takes root as Christ lives in the human soul and encouraged her to reflect on the truth of his words in her heart. As stated in other visions, the Christ Child also confirmed that a number of souls go without hearing his voice since they are preoccupied with themselves. He also stated that if someone's soul desired to hear his voice, this person would then reach a state of spiritual holiness in a relatively short time.

Padre Pío, OFMCap
Order of Friars Minor, Capuchin, Italy

Research still continues into the writings of Padre Pío (1887–1968) with regard to his spiritual inclination toward the Infant Jesus. He documented in his letters that he had visions of heavenly beings before entering the cloister. He describes the phenomenon as divine manifestations and explains that with his soul he sees heavenly secrets and divine attributes much better than seeing an image in a mirror. Among the visions, he describes the visit of the Virgin Mary with the Infant Jesus in her arms (July 1913). Padre Pío describes the Christ Child's face as more resplendent and luminous than the sun. He witnessed the Christ Child leave his mother's arms and hug a person in deep contemplative prayer. He added that the Infant Jesus also "kissed her an infinite number of times and bestowed upon her innumerable caresses."

The Child Jesus also arrived on a dark and cold night to console Padre Pío as he suffered evil torment. He describes his sensations when seeing the Infant Jesus: "Dear God! How my heart throbbed, how my cheeks burned while this heavenly Child was close to me!" (June 1912). In his relationship with the Infant Jesus, Padre Pío wrote that he was the plaything of the Child Jesus; however, he never considered himself worthy of any affection from the Christ Child. In a letter he wrote to Padre Agostino in 1917, his greeting spells out the emotion he felt following a vision on Christmas night: "May the heavenly Child arouse in your heart also all the holy emotions he made me feel during the holy night when he was laid in the poor little crib."

The Christ Child often consoled
Padre Pío as he suffered.

Gaucin (see p. 64)

Clay Infant in hay-filled crib
(see pp. 112-114)

Statue of Infant Jesus painted by Thérèse of Lisieux

Images of the Holy Child

VI

Look at Little Jesus

Images of the Holy Child

Helpful Child Jesus of Sarnen
Hilfreiche Sarner Jesuskind
Sarnen, Switzerland

An image known as the Helpful Child of Sarnen has been venerated for well over half a century in Switzerland. Even today, local
people and pilgrims come to pray through the intercession of the
little medieval *Jesuskind*. In the Lake Lucerne region, circled by
the magnificent Alps, he continues to shower his favors on those
who come to him in love and trust.

A Benedictine cloister was founded in the twelfth century in
Engelberg, and a house for women was added in 1190. A small
image of the Christ Child was listed as part of the property of the
nuns at this time, although the exact circumstances and date of its
acquisition are not known. Historical accounts in the monastery
tell that Queen Agnes of Hungary offered her royal hood and
dress to the image, already known as "miraculous" in 1318.

The Sarnen image is a carved wooden figure almost twenty
inches tall. The child holds his left hand to his heart and his right
hand holds a world globe on his raised knee. He is dressed in an
elaborate robe known as the "Agnes garment" since it, as well as a
frontal, was made from the dress that the queen had donated. It
is a sumptuous garment of red satin sprinkled with hundreds of
pieces of decorative metal including coins, letter forms, religious
symbols, decorative leaves, small plaques, spangles, heraldic

The Helpful Child Jesus of Sarnen

badges, and love tokens known as minne symbols. Some of these the nuns may have sewed on for decoration; others undoubtedly were presented as devotional offerings from grateful clients. The infant's dress is a precious piece of history as well as a work of art.

At one time, the legs of the Christ Child were straight, as he lay in his little cradle. An extant document written by one of the Benedictines in 1634 describes a fourteenth-century vision of one of the sisters that explains the image's current posture. One Christmas evening, a sick nun could not attend Mass so she asked that the little image of the Christ Child be brought to her cell. She began to pray in front of the little statue. It seemed to come alive and began shivering with the cold and crying for our sins. At this time the Christ Child pulled his right foot and leg toward his body in the position the statue has today. The document goes on to point out a deep meaning for the new posture. It is almost as if the Child is holding the world in his hand and with his hand on his heart is listening very closely to those who come to him and is giving them peace. The document concludes "in which year this happened, we do not know, but it is enough to know that it did."

News of the prodigy at the convent of Engelberg soon became known, and it became a popular place of pilgrimage. The nuns' cloister prospered, and at times there were three hundred nuns living there.

In 1349, the Black Death swept through Europe claiming the lives of over a hundred of the nuns of Engelberg in four months. The number of pilgrims decreased, and the devotion went through a period of decline. In 1449, a fire destroyed the cloister, which was rebuilt but not well. By 1615, only seven nuns remained. They established a new foundation in Sarnen, bringing their beloved *Jesulein* with them against the wishes of the abbot. Here, in the new St. Andrew monastery*, the Infant had his own altar and began again to receive those who came requesting his assistance. Here, too, a shower of graces began to fall in order to prove that God listens to the prayers of those who come to him in faith and childlike simplicity. The image's fame spread and he became known as the Helpful Little Jesus Boy of Sarnen.

---

* In 1882, three nuns from this monastery came to the United States and founded the Benedictine monastery of St. Gertrude in Idaho.

Holy Bell Ringer
Filzmooser Kindl
Filzmoos, Austria

The little church of Saints Peter and Paul of Filzmoos in the Altenmarkt district of Salzberg is a quiet place of worship. Here, pilgrims have come for centuries, from near and far, to venerate the Child of Filzmoos, a late-Gothic wooden statue of the Christ Child. Since 1961, it dominates the apse of the church from a golden aureola suspended in a hanging glass shrine, the work of the artist Jakob Adlhart.

The Holy Bell Ringer

The parish church has kept records of miraculous favors granted since 1705, but devotion to the little image is much older. Votive offerings from this century show that the child was appealed to in life-threatening dangers, epilepsy, insanity, blindness, diseases and accidents of children, and the plague, to name only a few. During the renovations of 1959–1961, these offerings were removed from the interior of the church and preserved elsewhere.

As early as 1772, the parish vicar deplored the fact that the early history of the devotion, up until 1705, had not been recorded but passed on only verbally. Most likely the devotion and the attendant pilgrimages originated about the middle of the fifteenth century. The statue is a rural Bavarian-style wood carving of that time period; this date would also correspond with the history of the erection of a church there in 1474. By 1507, records indicate that it was known as a "grace church," one where heavenly favors were regularly granted. Research indicates that during the 1600s there were over fifty popular shrines to the Holy Child in central and southern Europe. Only a few of these, including the one at Filzmoos, have been preserved.

The Filzmooser Kindl stands about thirty-three inches tall. It is carved from wood, gessoed, and painted. His feet are crossed, one above the other. His right hand is raised in a gesture of blessing. A small golden bell hangs from the fingers of this hand. He holds a golden globe of the world in his left hand. The gilded crown he wears probably dates from a later period. There is no written record of the origin of the crown. One legend has survived, however, which tells that when the crown was fastened on the head of the child, the head of the statue began to bleed.

The head of the image is slightly inclined. His large eyes are open and seem to look lovingly at those who gaze on him with reverence. His expression is half smiling and half serious. The image seems friendly and affectionate and inspires love and confidence for the young Child Jesus known far and wide as the Holy Bell Ringer.

His beautifully embroidered robes date from the early part of the twentieth century. He is dressed according to the season. He wears gold for Christmas, white for Easter, and red for Pentecost and the rest of the year.

The oral history of the Filzmooser Kindl tells that once, when the area was still mainly pastureland, two pious shepherds out with their flocks heard the lovely sound of a small bell. Following the sound, they came upon a fallen, half-dead tree. Hanging from one of the branches was a carved image of the Christ Child. A small bell hung from his raised fingers. Immediately they reported the surprising find to the responsible priest at Altmarkt. He followed them to the spot and took the image home with him. That night it disappeared, only to be found back in the place where the herdsmen had originally discovered it. Seeing this, it was taken to the nearby Peterskirchlein (St. Peter's Church), where it remains to this day.

Filzmoos was never one of the large pilgrimage sites. Many of the customs practiced there in the past no longer exist, but only the forms have changed—the pilgrims still come humbly to ask for the help of the Holy Child, and the Holy Child continues to let fall a shower of graces on those who come to him in loving trust.

Holy Child of Aracoeli
Bambino di Aracoeli
Rome, Italy

A crowned, jeweled, life-size figure of the Child Jesus is venerated in a special chapel at the Basilica of Santa Maria in the Aracoeli quarter of Rome. The statue is world-famous, and pilgrims flock

Holy Child of Aracoeli

to venerate it because of many reported miracles, favors, and answered prayers.

The statue of the Holy Bambino dates back to the end of the fifteenth century. It was carved from the wood of an olive tree from the Mount of Olives near Gethsemane by a pious Franciscan friar. A quaint tradition tells that the friar did not have the necessary paints to complete his work, and so the statue was miraculously finished by an angel. As the friar returned to Rome, a severe storm at sea caused him to throw the small case containing the statue overboard. The case floated to the port of Livorno in the wake of the ship.

In the Eternal City, the statue soon became famous for reported miracles and was treated with special honor. One day during the Christmas season, a noble Roman matron stole the statue and hid it carefully in her home. She became severely ill, and her confessor ordered her to return the statue. The legend continues that the statue left her house by itself during the night and returned to its place in the church as the bells of the basilica rang in joy at the miracle.

Rich gifts of gold and precious stones give testimony to the gratitude of the faithful for the innumerable graces received. A number of times attempts have been made to sacrilegiously despoil the statue. In 1798, Serafin Petrarca, a Roman citizen, paid a huge ransom to save the statue from being burned by Napoleon's troops.

Pregnant women often visit the Holy Bambino to receive a special blessing, and many return bringing their infants to be consecrated to the Divine Child. In the past, the statue was often divested of its golden trappings and carried to the bedside of the sick faithful. At one time, Santo Bambino even had his own coach for his journeys.

Pope Leo XIII and the Vatican Chapter ordered the coronation of the image, which took place with a solemn ritual in 1897.

At Christmas, a special crèche is set up in the church. In one of the most famous nativity scenes of the world, the Infant is sometimes placed in the lap of a statue of the Virgin. Other times he is placed in a crib. Throughout the season, the children of Rome come to sing, recite poems, and perform playlets for the Infant King. At dusk on the feast of the Epiphany, in a special ceremony, a blessing is given to the pilgrims gathered on the Capitoline Hill.

The medieval image of the Holy Bambino was stolen and recovered twice. It was stolen again in 1994 and has not been recovered, so it has been replaced by a copy, which is venerated in its place.

Holy Child of Cebu
Santo Niño de Cebu
Cebu, Philippines

A small wooden statue of the Holy Child known as Santo Niño
of Cebu is the beloved patron of the Filipino people. They consider him the prime missionary to their country, the only Catholic
country of the Orient.

The Legazpi-Urdaneta expedition arrived in the Philippines
at Cebu on April 27, 1565. On landing, Legazpi's soldiers began
to make a house-to-house inspection of the homes of the burned-
out city. The following day Juan Camus, one of the sailors in the
fleet, found in a modest home a small pine box that held a painted
wooden image of the Holy Child Jesus. It was resting in its original gilded cradle and was quite well preserved, although the face
had darkened because of the tropical climate. The only item
remaining of its original Spanish clothing was a small velvet hat;
otherwise it was dressed in a simple native shirt.

The image was taken to a provisional chapel where the
Augustinian Fray Andres de Urdaneta celebrated a Mass in
thanksgiving for the success of the expedition and for the mission
to Christianize the islands. Fray Urdaneta observed that the image
was like those made in Flanders (present-day northern France and
western Belgium). Here, during the sixteenth century talented
wood-carvers met Spain's demand for the popular statues of the
Christ Child depicted as king. The Infant of Cebu is believed to
be the image that Magellan brought from Spain forty-four years
earlier. The chaplain of Magellan's expedition, Father Pedro
Valderrama, gave the little statue to Rajah Humabon's wife, the
tribal queen Juana, on her conversion to Christianity in 1521, the
day she was baptized.

Only twelve inches tall, the little statue stands on a carved
bronze base and is protected by a glass bell decorated with gold

and precious gems. He wears regal clothing of jewel-studded liturgical garments. Like the Infant of Prague, which became famous in Europe a century later, the Child of Cebu holds a globe with a cross in one hand. In the other hand, he holds a scepter and a pilgrim's staff. Two fingers of that hand are raised in blessing. Today he wears a golden crown set with diamonds over his carved wooden curls, instead of the modest little cap he wore when he was found by Juan Camus. On special feast days, he wears a cummerbund set with antique Spanish gold coins. Diamonds and emeralds decorate the delicate gold chains he wears and his boots are studded with pearls. Members of the local *cofradia,* or confraternity, change the infant's clothing on traditional celebration dates. Since people expect special blessings when the statue wears handmade clothing, the Infant of Cebu routinely wears a number of undergarments of lace and silk.

So many miracles became associated with the little image that, in the seventeenth century, King Charles III of Spain awarded it the Toison de Oro, or the Golden Fleece. During the celebration held to commemorate the fourth centennial of the Christianization of the Philippines, then Prince Juan Carlos, later Spain's king, gifted it with a golden crown.

The convent of the Santo Niño was built by Fray Urdaneta himself in 1565, close to the place where Magellan had planted his cross. It was the first convent in the Philippines. In the same year an urbanization plan for the city was set and a place for the church and convent of San Agustín was allocated. The spot is believed to be the same spot where the image of the Santo Niño was found. Historians believe that at least three churches were built there before the present one. The church that stands today was constructed in 1735. It was elevated to the rank of minor basilica in 1965. In 1975, the Augustinian Fathers built a marble chapel inside the basilica to serve as a shrine for the little figure of Santo Niño.

Santo Niño de Cebu

In 1567, the first European–Asian marriage took place inside a makeshift chapel during the fiesta of the Santo Niño of Cebu. The bride was a young, beautiful niece of Rajah Tupas. The bridegroom was the Greek master carpenter of Legazpi's expedition, Andres Calafata. The *adelantado* Legazpi acted as *ninong*, or godfather. The love affair started when Tupas's niece was sent to the convent to receive Christian formation, there, she was baptized and given the name Isabel. While there, she met the Greek carpenter and they fell in love.

This wedding ushered in mutual friendship between the two cultures, and peace and understanding were achieved with these first two ambassadors of goodwill. Their wedding ceremony is reenacted every year during the feast of Santo Niño, and jubilantly celebrated with food, dances, and fireworks to recall the happiness and good omen brought about to the Cebuanos when Princess Isabella married Maestro Andres.

During World War II, the church where the image was kept was damaged by American bombing. The image, however, was found hanging by its clothes, intact and unharmed. Enshrined in his chapel at the basilica, the Santo Niño image has counterparts and replicas all over the Islands. In addition, there are many other "named images" of the Christ Child, each with its own story, throughout the country. A perpetual novena to the Holy Child of Cebu was begun at this shrine by the Augustinian Fathers in 1958.

Santo Niño of Cebu in the United States

In a number of cities in the United States where there is a large Filipino population, it has become popular to celebrate the feast of Santo Niño with the traditional procession and dances.

The Cofradia del Santo Niño de Cebu was formed in the Houston, Texas, area in 1987. Three small statues belonging to

Celebration in honor of Santo Niño of Cebu

the confraternity are pilgrim statues that travel from home to home, staying a week or two in each. The visits of the little pilgrim provide an opportunity for the parents to teach their children about the faith. Catholic parenting and strong family ties have kept the Filipino community pious and committed Catholics.

The *cofradia* holds an annual celebration in honor of the Christ Child at Holy Family Church in Missouri City on the last Saturday of January. The day begins with the recitation of the rosary in the church, which is led by children of the Santo Niño devotees. Then everyone lines up in front of the church behind a large statue of Santo Niño carried on a decorated platform by four men. The people carry their home images of the Christ Child and each holds a red or gold balloon. To the insistent tap of a snare drum, the procession begins and winds its way around the church property. Once back at the entrance to the church, the people gather close and a priest asks a special blessing. With a joyful cry of "¡Viva Santo Niño, Pit Señor!"* the balloons are released heavenward.

Then the devotees enter the church for Mass, placing their Niños on tables at the back of the room to await the blessing of the celebrant. In addition to images of the Cebu Christ Child in all sizes and materials, there are many other representations of the Christ Child. The Infant of Prague and the Divino Niño of Colombia are present. One, dressed as a Filipino farmer, is called the Palaboy, or Wanderer. The Palaboy is believed to roam around, testing the charity of the people he encounters. Santo Niño de Tondo, Santo Niño Suerte, and Santo Niño Pescador are among the many others represented here.

After the Mass, there are blessing ceremonies for the children, for married couples, and for the home images of the Santo Niño. Then, all are invited to continue the celebration in the parish hall where delicious Filipino food is served and the traditional *sinulog* dance is performed in honor of the Holy Child.

Beneath all his regal trappings, the little Child of Cebu represents the innocence of the Christ Child, and devotion to him brings forth the joy and happiness of the Catholic faith.

Holy Child of Gaucín
Santo Niño de Gaucín
Gaucín, Spain

For nearly five hundred years, the citizens of Gaucín, Spain, have celebrated an image of the Holy Child. The gift of a saint, it was the Holy Child himself who directed the saint to present it as a remembrance of his appearance there.

---

*No exact translation of the phrases is possible. They are joyful exclamations. The first, in Spanish, roughly is translated as "Long live the Holy Child"; the second is a combination of Tagalog and Spanish and is similar to saying "Hoorah for Jesus."

The traditional story of the Holy Child of Gaucín was written down at the end of the nineteenth century by Don Ubaldo de Molina Fernández, the official historian of Gaucín. It tells that one summer day in 1536, an itinerant Portuguese bookseller, Juan Ciudad, was walking to Gaucín, carrying a heavy load of religious books.

The vicissitudes of life had buffeted Juan, who could not decide his true path in life. At times it seemed clear; at others his way was obscure. He had worked as a shepherd, a soldier, and a bricklayer, always being charitable and kind, before he began to sell religious books from town to town. Nearly forty years old, his desire to give his life to God was growing stronger, but Juan could not see exactly what God wanted him to do.

The oppressive heat and the heavy load were aggravated by the uneven road on the way from Gibraltar to Gaucín. About halfway on his journey, nearly to an area the locals called the Adelfilla, Juan was startled to see someone walking ahead of him on the solitary mountain road. It was a pretty boy in poor clothes; the child had no shoes and was walking along the rocky road barefoot.

Thinking that the little boy was lost and worried that the rocks would tear the tender little feet to pieces, Juan, with more charity than thought, offered the child his hemp sandals. Thanking him, the boy refused the offering since the man's sandals were much too large for his tiny feet.

The innocence and extraordinary beauty of the child fascinated and attracted Juan, who said, "Precious little boy and brother, if my sandals are not acceptable to you, then accept the service of my shoulders. Your value before God is worth much more than these books." Saying this, and in order to prove his words, Juan bent down and lowered his head so the child could climb on. As the young boy climbed onto his shoulders, Juan straightened up and walked proudly on, happy for the rest he was giving to such an astonishingly lovely child.

A little while later, Juan began to feel as St. Christopher once had: as if he had the world on his shoulders. His light load began to grow very heavy, and he weakened and began to lean heavily on his walking stick. Just at the Adelfilla, there was a little spring, which still flows today. Juan said to the child, "precious boy and brother, give me a minute to drink a little water and to rest as I have worked up a sweat." Carefully, he set the child down in the shade of a tree. He went to the spring and drank thirstily. On his return, he was pleasantly surprised to hear the child calling to him. Suddenly, he saw in the poor boy the greatness and majesty of the Incarnate Word. The Christ Child handed him an open pomegranate, crowned with his cross, and told him, "You will be called John of God, and Granada will be your cross, and through it you will see me in Glory. As testimony of my appearance, give to Gaucín an image that represents me as a child." Then the beautiful child disappeared into the pearly clouds.

After this apparition, Juan Ciudad left his doubts in the Adelfilla and followed with his whole heart what the Holy Child had directed. In Granada, he dedicated the rest of his life to helping the needy and giving succor and protection to the sick. His daily example brought about the creation of a work that even today continues the steps of the founder in charity—the Brothers Hospitalers of St. John of God. Saint John of God (1495–1550) was canonized in 1690.

But what of the image promised by the Christ Child to Gaucín in proof of John's vision?

Following the directive of the divine voice, John traveled to Alhambra to begin his work. One day, in Andalusia on a trip to collect funds for the poor, John acquired a little statue of the Christ Child. On arriving at the city of Ronda, he charitably exchanged his clothes with a poor soldier, and in that disguise, carrying the carefully wrapped sacred image, he entered the Hermitage of the Incarnation at the Castle of Águila one September day in 1546. Silently he entered the church and placed the little statue on the altar, completing the design of Divine Providence.

Since that day, the citizens of Gaucín have been ardent in their service and devotion to the Christ Child. The story of the image has been passed down from generation to generation, and each year since the first anniversary of the gift, the traditional festival in honor of the Christ Child is held on September 8.

All that remains of the original image is a photo made in 1920. The picture confirms the description of the only written document that remains. The child is dressed in a simple tunic. His left hand holds a little world globe of crystal and his right is raised in blessing. The beautiful image is considered a marvel of Christian art and is most likely from the Seville school of art founded in the middle of the sixteenth century by Pedro Torrigiano.

In 1810, the little image was thrown away during one of the French raids. First, it was robbed of its rich clothing and expensive votive offerings, which were taken and sold. It was struck in the face with a bayonet and thrown down in the rocks around the castle where it lay hidden for two years. Fortunately, it was found by a pious woman, Mrs. Ana Jimenez-Orozco, who restored it. Once again the little image was venerated during the September fiestas for the rest of the nineteenth century and the first part of the twentieth.

During the first days of the bloody Spanish Civil War, the image disappeared. Two stories of its fate are given. One holds that the statue was burned; the other says that a devotee of the Holy Child took it to safety. Some people still hope that one day the precious image will return.

In September 1937, the Brothers of St. John of God of Granada donated an image of the Holy Child to the parish of San

Sebastian. They had acquired the wooden statue in an antique shop in Granada. This image was used until the 1960s when the pastor, Father Juan Jiménez Higueras, obtained a new statue for the hermitage, which is the one in use today.

The festival continues today as one of the most important feasts of the year in Gaucín. On the evening of September 7, the statues of the Christ Child and of St. John of God are taken from the hermitage to the parochial church of San Sebastian where a Mass is held in commemoration of the apparition of the Christ Child to St. John of God. After the liturgical celebration, the people feast and dance throughout the evening. On the following day, the celebration begins again at dawn. The people attend Mass in pious thanksgiving for all the graces they have received. All day, people come to the church to venerate the Holy Child and the great Portuguese saint. At about five in the afternoon, the images leave the church and are carried in procession through nearly all the streets of the town, accompanied by music and large numbers of people, carrying lighted candles and singing to the Holy Child. At eight thirty, after returning to the church of San Sebastian, the procession accompanies the Holy Child back to the hermitage. Five centuries of tradition have held that between those walls of stone and adobe lies the place where the saint of Granada encountered the Holy Child. Since that blessed day, the people of the area have kept the love of the Child Jesus in their hearts, considering him their defender and their help in all their needs.

Today's festival is very similar to those that have been carried out since 1536. The only exception is that an additional celebration has been added on the last Sunday of August, which has been held for the past forty years. In 1960, the confraternity of the Holy Child inaugurated a hermitage at the place of the apparition.

Boy of the Town
Niñopan, Niñopa
Xochimilco, Mexico

Unlike other famous statues of the Christ Child who preside from altars in chapels, churches, and basilicas, Niñopan is so much a part of the hearts of the people that he lives not in a church but in the homes of his devotees.

Each year after Candelaria (February 2, feast of the Presentation) the Niñopan is taken from the *mayordomos,* or stewards, of the previous year and given to the new guardians.

Niñopan

In the sixteenth century, an Indian convert named Martin Cortes de Alvarado, built a small chapel near Xochimilco. He obtained a sculpture of the Child Jesus made in the workshop of the Franciscans at the Convent of St. Bernard of Sienna. The image was sculpted by an indigenous Xochimilcan and became known as Niñopan. Niñopa, or Niñopan, is a word composed of the Spanish for child (*niño*) and the Nahualt, the native language of the area, for town or place. At first called *señor de los indios* (Lord of the Indians), it later became known as Niñopa or Niñopan.

On Alvarado's death, he willed the statue to a relative, who, on his own death, willed it to another. This began the tradition of mayordomos as stewards or guardians of the image. Since the people were accustomed to obeying the mayordomo, the stewards told them to pray to the Niñopan for miracles, and many began to say that their requests were granted. The Franciscans used the little image to spread the gospel, and some writers say that it was at one time connected with the *cofradias,* or religious brotherhoods.

Niñopan is sculpted of colorin wood and cornstalk paste. It was sculpted so it could sit or lie down. One of his hands is raised in blessing. Only about eight inches tall, the statue has brown eyes of crystal, with dark eyelashes and natural hair.

At one time, the parish priest of Xochimilco wanted to disregard the traditions and take the statue to the church with the other saints, over the objection of the mayordomo and the people. A lawsuit was brought and while it was being decided, the parishioners refused to attend the church, going instead to nearby churches. The case was decided in favor of tradition with the stipulation that should the tradition be broken, the image would be given to the Secretariat of National Patrimony. There is little danger of this since prospective mayordomos are already on the list until 2035.

Niñopan is treated as if he were a real child. Each day he is dressed in beautiful outfits and at night he is undressed and laid in a little bed. During the year, this little pilgrim of the barrios goes out to visit the sick, in the hospitals and in their homes. On February 2, he is taken to bless the fields, in keeping with the agricultural basis of the area. Toys are a favorite ex-voto offering at his altar; on the feast of the Three Kings, he is showered with all manner of toys. Some say that he will play with them the following night. The toys are then distributed to poor children.

Just as any normal child, Niñopan can be mischievous. Some say he gets up at night to play or to creep into the cornfield to see how the corn is growing. He returns the following morning with his little shoes covered with mud. Others tell that when he is angry his cheeks blush, and when he is happy his eyes brighten and he smiles.

During the Cristero rebellion and the persecution of the church in Mexico, the people hid him from the soldiers, knowing they would try to destroy the beloved little image. Niñopan gained the reputation of having the power to appear and disappear and became a patron for the Catholic soldiers.

To be selected mayordomo is considered a great honor in spite of the enormous cost. Some couples are on the list for thirty or forty years before their turn to host the little image arrives. During the year they are guardians, they give up their regular work in order to host Niñopan and to accompany him to visit the sick and to attend the festivals of the area. All of the barrios of the area are visited throughout the year. Two rooms are set aside in their home; usually the living room and the kitchen. The rooms are decorated with flowers and candles and food is freely given to all who come to pray before the little image. Anyone is welcome as long as they are reverent. The workday of the little Niño and his mayordomo is from seven in the morning to seven thirty at night. There are attendants at Mass, prayers, and visits. The

December festivities are planned years in advance. The Niño is carried around to the Posadas, a reenactment of St. Joseph and Our Lady's attempt to find shelter in Bethlehem. Each day there is a party in a different house. The party begins at seven in the morning and ends in the wee hours of the following morning when the Niñopan is accompanied by a procession back to the home of the mayordomo.

As he goes among his people, the Niñopan seems to work to unite families in love. The mayordomos say their stewardship is important because all they do for Niñopan is done for God. The image known as the Child of the Place stands in place, as a physical representation, of our unseen God.

Infant Jesus of Prague
Prague, Czech Republic

A venerable little image known as the Infant of Prague is arguably the most famous statue of the Christ Child in the world. Fondly called the "Little King," devotion to the infancy under this title has spread around the globe.

In 1556, Maria Manriquez de Lara of Spain brought the statue, a precious family heirloom, with her to Bohemia (now the Czech Republic) when she married the Czech nobleman Vratislav of Pernstyn. Made in Spanish Baroque style, the statue is eighteen inches tall, carved of wood, and thinly coated with wax. The left hand holds a miniature globe surmounted by a cross. The right hand is extended in the form of the papal blessing. In keeping with the Baroque custom of dressing holy images, since the early part of the eighteenth century, the Little King is dressed according to the liturgical season. In order to protect its fragile wax surface, up to the waist the image is encased in a silver case. He has an extensive wardrobe of clothes, and the original garments he wore when he arrived in Bohemia have been preserved.

Infant Jesus of Prague

Princess Polyxena Lobkowitz received the statue as a wedding gift from her mother, and in 1628 she presented the statue to the discalced Carmelites of Prague, telling them, prophetically, that as long as they honored the Child Jesus as king and venerated his image, they would not lack what they needed. Her prediction was verified, and as long as the Divine Infant's image was honored, the community prospered, spiritually and temporally.

At the monastery, the image was placed in the chapel and honored with daily devotions. One of the novices, Cyril of the Mother of God (Nicholas Schokwilerg, d. 1675), developed a deep devotion and later became the indefatigable apostle of the Little King.

In 1631, the Swedish anti-Catholic forces of King Gustavus Adolphus invaded Prague and plundered the city, including the monastery. The holy image was thrown in a heap of rubbish behind the high altar where it remained for a number of years. In 1637, Father Cyrillus returned to Prague, searched for and found the little image. He repaired it and renewed the devotions.

Reported miracles and favors multiplied. The image became known as a thaumaturge and was often called the Miraculous Infant of Prague. In 1655, the statue was solemnly crowned in a special coronation ceremony by the supreme burgrave of the Czech kingdom.

Nearly a century later, in 1739, the Carmelites of the Austrian Province chose to promote the devotion as part of their apostolate. In l741, the Little King was moved to a magnificent shrine on the epistle side of the Church of Our Lady of Victory. Throughout the eighteenth century, the popularity of the Infant of Prague began to spread throughout the world. Pope Leo XIII indulgenced the devotion in 1896, and Pope Pius X approved a confraternity under the guidance of the Carmelites, which increased the spread of the devotion in the twentieth century. The shrine in Prague has become one of the most famous and popular shrines in the world.

The Shrine in the United States

In the United States, there is a canonically established national shrine to the Infant Jesus of Prague at Prague, Oklahoma. The area was settled by Czech immigrants in the late 1800s and a church established under the patronage of St. Wenceslaus was built in 1903. Later a small brick church was built that by the 1940s was in need of repair or replacement, but the parish did not have the resources to build a new church. In 1947, the pastor, Father George V. Johnson, received a statue of the Little King from the Sisters of Mercy in Bakersville, California. Father Johnson put the statue in the back of his church along with some material about the devotion. In his own prayers, Father Johnson promised to set up a shrine to the Holy Child if the Infant would help with building the new church. Within two years, the dream of a new church became a reality. Pope Pius XII approved the shrine's erection as a national shrine and it was dedicated in February 1949.

*Shrine to the Infant Jesus of Prague,
United States*

Shrines in Italy and Spain

Two other famous centers of devotion to the Infant of Prague, where the images are termed "miraculous" because of the great number of favors reported, are located in Arenzano, Italy, and in Barcelona, Spain.

In 1889, Father Leopoldo Beccaro founded a Carmelite monastery at Arenzano near Genoa, Italy. Here the Holy Child

*Infant Jesus of Prague
at the Shrine in
Arenzano, Italy*

*Shrine to Infant Jesus
of Prague in Barcelona,
Spain*

was venerated in a small chapel until 1905 when the splendid church was built to accommodate the increasing devotion to the Holy Child. A replica of the Prague statue was donated in 1902 and became affectionately known as the Great Little King. The image was crowned in 1924 with a golden crown donated by Pope Pius XI. The globe held by this image is gold, a gift of gratitude from the citizens of Arenzano in thanks for being spared in the Nazi bombing of the city in 1944.

The cult of the Child Jesus of Prague began to be celebrated in Spain at the end of the nineteenth century by the Salesas, Visitations nuns of Barcelona who began the devotion here. During the religious persecution in 1936, the statue was saved by the Muntadas family, who wrapped it in curtains and hid it in a trunk.

Although each of these famous images of the Little King of Prague has seen times of trial, it has always escaped from harm and the devotion has continued to spread. Copies of the miraculous statue are treasured in churches, religious houses, and homes throughout the world. The more the Christ Child is honored, the more he blesses those who come before him in prayer.

Boy Mayor
El Niño Alcalde
La Rioja, Argentina

A unique double procession has been celebrated at the turn of the year in the province of La Rioja, Argentina, for over four hundred years. Known as the *tinkunaco,* or encounter, the image of the patron saint of the area, St. Nicholas of Bari, comes to meet the image of the Christ Child, known as the Niño Alcalde, and renders homage to the Son of God. The festival celebrates the peace pact of the Spaniards and the indigenous peoples in 1593.

The Boy Mayor

The image of the patron saint leaves his home in the cathedral at about eleven in the morning on December 31, accompanied by a colorful procession of devotees. This is the traditional day on which, in colonial times, there was a change of the Spanish authorities of the area.

At the same time, the procession with the Niño Alcalde starts off from his customary altar at the Church of St. Francis. Dressed in the black velvet suit, cape, and hat of a Spanish alcalde and carrying the scepter of justice in his little hand, he is borne aloft by twelve men wearing suits, ties, and the colorful scapulars and headbands symbolizing the devotion of the indigenous people to the Holy Child. Other devotees join the procession. The women wear flowers and ribbons in colorful hues. The children wear a small black votive cape with yellow and gold trim in request and in gratitude for favors from the Christ Child. Along the way, there is music and singing.

The processions meet at noon in front of the House of Government, or city hall. Here the encounter takes place. Accompanied by special prayers and verses, the image of St. Nicholas is inclined three times in front of the Christ Child, who remains motionless. The procession is symbolic of the native peoples' submission to God, "the Mayor of the World," as their leader. The reverences are made humbly and with hymns of praise to God and to the Virgin Mary.

After the *tinkunaco,* both images are taken to the cathedral where they remain together, receiving the loving devotion of the town, until January 3. That day, St. Nicholas says goodbye to the Niño Alcalde, again in front of the town hall, and the image of the little alcalde is carried back to the church of St. Francis while that of the saint returns to the cathedral.

The statue of the Niño Alcalde is almost twenty-three inches tall in a standing position and is carved of wood, gessoed and painted. It has long blonde curls of natural hair and a smiling face with rosy cheeks and brilliant blue eyes. The statue represents the Christ Child at about the age of six or seven years and wears the elegant clothing of a Spanish alcalde, including a doublet of rich jet velvet, a sword, and a hat with arched black feathers. His right hand is raised in blessing, and his left hand holds a silver stick that ends with the cross of Caravaca. On the day of the *tinkunaco,* the image is adorned with beautiful jewels, chains, and a watch, which have been presented to him by grateful clients in thanksgiving for favors received. The image appears to have been made in the "Cuzqueña school," which reaffirms the theory that the image was brought from Peru. In the Iglesia de la Merced in Cuzco, Peru, there is another ancient image of the Jesus Alcalde that is venerated there. This, too, reaffirms the theory that the image and devotion may have been brought by St. Francis Solano

(1549–1610), the great saint (canonized in 1726) and defender of the indigenous peoples of the area.

In 1593, a large group of Indians surrounded La Rioja and threatened to kill all the Spaniards and Christianized Indians. St. Francis went out to meet them, playing his violin and carrying the image of the Christ Child dressed as a Spanish alcalde. He spoke to them in their native language and disarmed them, moving their hearts with his kindness. They began to venerate the image, and nine thousand people begged him for instructions and were baptized. Since that time, the people of La Rioja have acclaimed the little alcalde as "Mayor of the World" and the patron of their town.

Holy Child of the Thorn
El Niño de la Espina
Cuzco, Peru

Jesuit missionaries arrived in Peru in 1568, bringing along their love of the Holy Child. Two centuries-old paintings, one of which has now disappeared, represent the boy Jesus standing with his hand raised in blessing and his other hand holding a globe, wearing the clothing of an Inca. They are obviously portraits of polychrome images of the Christ Child, images of syncretization and acculturation that mediate between the visible and the invisible world.

In the Jesuit Chronicle of 1600 for the province of Peru, there is mention of a church built on the old palace of the Inca Huayna Capac in 1571 in Cuzco. Here the Jesuits established a brotherhood of Indians dedicated to the name of Jesus, which operated in over a hundred towns in the area. Over the next two centuries, in spite of native resistance, the Inca culture was assimilated into the Spanish Catholic empire, and the Inca sun god was overcome by the God Son. Images of the new Son of Justice bore the monogram JHS (Jesus Homini Salvator), the acronym of the holy name of Jesus and the primary emblem of the Jesuit Order, and were dressed like the Inca, the son of the sun who had become the Son, Savior of the World.

From the time the boy God entered the Andes, Peruvians embraced him with loving open arms. Here the Christ Child is known by the name Manuelito, a familiar use of the name Emmanuel. The prodigies the Holy Child did in each town are legion. These legends have resulted in numerous specific titles and images of the little Manuelito.

Holy Child of the Thorn

Perhaps the most famous of the Manuelitos of Cuzco is El Niño de la Espina, the Child of the Thorn. Sitting in a regally carved wooden chair, the image is dressed in native attire. His hat displays red tassels, symbolic of his kingship. In his left hand, he holds a thorn in the shape of a cross; his right foot is bloody. The pious legend of this charming image dates back to colonial times. One day, the image of the Christ Child in the chapel leaped from its mother's arms and, barefoot, went out into the countryside to search for some pretty colored rocks. At the same time, a group of three shepherd children were tending their sheep when one of the sheep became lost. While they were searching for their sheep, they came across a little Inca child, sitting in a chair, crying because he had a thorn in his foot. With great pity, the little shepherds helped the little Inca, taking the thorn from his foot. In return, the little boy helped them search for and recover their lost sheep. The little Inca then disappeared. News of the prodigy spread, an image was sculpted, and a cult grew up around the statue, which became known as the Child of the Thorn.

Child Jesus of Loreto
Loretokindlein
Salzburg, Austria

One of the greatest treasures of the Loreto convent of the Capuchin nuns in Salzburg is a centuries-old statue of Jesus, known as the miraculous Child Jesus of Loreto. Standing only four inches tall, the delicate image is carved of ivory. The face has a fine line through it as if it had once been broken. Today, the statue has no color at all, but old writings indicate that at one time its hair was gold and the eyes and mouth were painted. The artist is unknown, but the statue's history dates to 1620 when it was given as a gift to Mother Euphrasia of the Capuchin convent in Ensisheim, Switzerland.

There was a cloister of Capuchin monks in nearby Ensisheim, and one of the monks, Father John Chrysostom Schenk, begged Mother Euphrasia to give the little *Jesuslein* to him. She agreed on condition that he return it to the nuns when he died. Father Chrysostom dressed the little image in a simple robe of violet blue with a white collar and a red sash. He put a forget-me-not in the child's right hand and a cross in the left hand. The flower served as a reminder of his love for the Child Jesus and the cross as a reminder that the Son of God became man to later be crucified for our sake.

Father Chrysostom loved the little image and carried it everywhere with him to spread the love of the Christ Child. Eventually he took it to Salzburg. He had a little box, known as a *stammauschen,* or "traveling home," made of wood and lined with red silk to carry the statue in. The cover of the box was made to slide off, and the sides were decorated with angels. The original box is preserved at Salzburg, although in 1742 it was covered in silver by a grateful relative. The priest's devotion to the infancy was so well known that he earned the nickname "Christkindle-Pater," or "Father Christchild."

The pious priest developed a very personal devotion to the Christ Child through the image and, as well as praying before it, he spoke with it as if it were his best friend and companion. Father Chrysostom told a number of stories about the image. Once, while adoring Christ in front of the image, the bell rang to summon the monks to prayer. Kissing the little statue, he placed it on a shelf in his room and said "take care of yourself" as he left. On his return, he found that the statue had fallen and smashed to pieces. Tearfully he showed the other monks what had happened. He tried to put the pieces together but could not. As the midday lunch bell rang, he left again, saying, "You, lovely child, should have been more careful. I know of no one who can mend you so, if it be God's will, I leave you to mend yourself." On his return,

Child Jesus of Loreto

he discovered to his joy that the statue was whole again with no trace of any crack or line to mar it. Happily he called the monks to see the prodigy of God's blessing on his servant.

Another time, while on a trip in 1625, Father Chrysostom fell and dropped the statue, which cracked from its head to its waist. He took it to a sculptor who sadly reported that there was nothing he could do to mend the little image. He took the broken pieces home, and prayed before and comforted the Christ Child; in the morning it was whole again. Taking the statue back to the sculptor, he showed the way that God had answered his prayer. The sculptor was so impressed by the miracle that he entered the monastery. The statue was broken and repaired a third time, but a hairline fracture remains until this day

At one time, Father Chrysostom and the father provincial visited the same cloister. Fearing that the pious priest's devotion was excessive and that it would disturb the peace of the cloister, the provincial took it from him and returned to Freiburg, where he intended to give the image to a wealthy patron. That night, he put the image in his cell, but in the morning it had disappeared. The image had returned by itself to Salzburg.

Father Chrysostom continued to make the devotion of the Christ Child known, and when asked would lend the image to the pious. Many miraculous cures and favors were reported by the local faithful.

When Father Chrysostom died, Mother Euphrasia was traveling and did not hear of his passing. The father provincial took the little statue and gave it to his sister at the cloister of Dieffendorf. By chance, Mother Euphrasia stopped for the night at this same cloister. When the provincial's sister learned who she was, she cried out "Oh no, you have come to take my image of the Baby Jesus!" Seeing her devotion, Mother Euphrasia agreed to lend the image to her for a while and returned to Salzburg without it. After six years, the provincial's sister died, but the statue was not returned. Instead it was placed on a special altar in Dieffendorf. Only after a second request was made was the statue returned to its rightful owner.

The Loretokindlein is dressed in rich robes and covered with precious jewels, the gifts of grateful clients in thanksgiving for favors received. One dress was handmade of red velvet and decorated with pearls by the Empress Elizabeth in 1754. The statue was not always dressed so richly; at first he was given the simplest of robes.

Today, the sisters in Salzburg continue to promote the devotion to the Christ Child. They make and dress replicas of the miraculous Child of Loreto to help raise the funds needed to support their monastery.

Little King of Grace
L'Enfant-Jésus de Beaune
Beaune, France

The statue known as the Little King of Grace was a Christmas gift in 1643 to the Venerable Sister Margaret of the Blessed Sacrament (1619–1648) from the pious layman Baron Gaston de Renty.

In 1630, an eleven-year-old orphan girl named Margaret Parigot entered the Carmelite monastery of Beaune, one of the first of the reformed Carmels in France. She took her vows in 1636 at the age of seventeen. A mystic and a victim soul, Margaret was devoted to the infancy of Christ. In a series of private revelations, the Child Jesus instructed her to promote the devotion to his infancy and taught her a number of pious practices that he wished to make known to the world, including a chaplet, the commemoration of his birth on the twenty-fifth of each month, and the plan for an association dedicated in his honor, which came to fruition in the form of a confraternity.

Margaret's reputation soon became known outside of Carmel. She predicted the safety of the city of Beaune in 1636 during an invasion of Burgundy. She told her prioress, "The Infant Jesus has told me that the city will be safe." King Louis XIII and Queen Anne had been married twenty-three years but remained childless. Margaret assured the Queen that she would bear an heir to the

Little King of France

throne, and the birth of Louis XIV in 1638 was seen as a divine gift by his parents.

Margaret attracted the attention of the Servant of God Father John Jacob Olier (1608-1657) and the pious layman Baron Gaston de Renty (1611-1649) who became friends and helpers in the promotion of devotion to the Christ Child. Father Olier, the founder of the Sulpicians, established a seminary in 1641. Priests went from this seminary and zealously spread the devotion to the Child Jesus throughout France. After a visit to Margaret in 1643,

Baron de Renty was inflamed with the love of the Holy Infancy. Returning home, he sent her the image of the Little King. The statue is carved from wood and made with movable joints so that it can be dressed. It is attributed to the work of the Baron himself, who was known to have made and presented a number of works of art to poor churches. The crowned image has a large collection of sumptuous clothing, is decorated with jewels and crowned. A convert to Catholicism, Baron de Renty founded the Society of the Blessed Sacrament and became one of the most ardent promoters of the devotion to the Holy Child.

To honor the Christ Child, Sister Margaret obtained the superior's permission to construct a little chapel next to the Carmel. Donations poured in and the chapel was erected in 1639. The original image honored in the chapel was a stone image of the Virgin holding the Holy Child; later, Baron de Renty's sculpture was placed there. Soon pilgrims began to come to the little chapel. Both the wealthy aristocracy and the humble poor were attracted to visit the image of the Little King of Grace. The pilgrimages lasted until the French Revolution, when the statue was safely hidden and later returned to the nuns who kept it in their enclosure. The chapel, however, had been destroyed.

In 1873, the image was again displayed to the public in the chapel of the monastery. Supplicants began to come to visit the Little King, privately and in groups. A large correspondence poured into the monastery with poignant requests for prayers and thanks for graces received. The walls of the little chapel became covered with ex votos, and certain forms of devotion instituted by Sister Margaret were maintained there. Booklets distributed to the faithful explained that devotion to the Infant Jesus originated with Christ himself, who called us to become like little children to attain the Kingdom of Heaven (Matthew 18:3).

The Carmel of Beaune closed in 2001 and the nuns moved to other monasteries of the order. The little image, however,

remains in the ancient chapel of the former convent at 14 rue de
Chorey, which is now in charge of the Community of the Beati-
tudes of Beaune.

Holy Child of Atocha
Santo Niño de Atocha
Fresnillo, Mexico

Portrayed as a young Spanish pilgrim, the image of the Child
Jesus known as Santo Niño de Atocha is dressed in a long gown
with a cape that has a wide lace collar and frilled cuffs. The traditional symbol of a pilgrim, a cockleshell, adorns his cape, and he
holds a little basket in his left hand and a water gourd suspended
from a staff in his right hand. The little Christ Child wears buck-
led sandals—huaraches—of silver, and a large, floppy hat with a
feather. Although he is known as a wanderer, he is usually shown
seated in a little chair.

The pious tradition of Santo Niño de Atocha is a story rich
in both history and popular devotion. Although the Holy Child
is the miracle worker, the devotion was originally to the Virgin
Mary. As is proper, before a child is asked to do something, first
the petitioner must ask permission from his mother. Thus, the
prayers and novenas to the Infant of Atocha begin with a prayer
to Mary, Our Lady of Atocha.

Tradition says devotion to Our Lady of Atocha and her
wonder-working child originated in Antioch and that St. Luke
the Evangelist was the sculptor of the first mother-and-child
image. Thus the word *Atocha* could be another form of Antioch.
Devotion to Our Lady under this name spread rapidly, and by
1162 a beautiful medieval statue was in Toledo in the Church of
St. Leocadia. In 1523, Charles V of Spain commissioned an enormous temple and placed the statue under the care of the Domini-

cans. The image of the Divine Child was detachable, and devout families would borrow the image of the infant when a woman was near the time of childbirth.

The pious legend of the wonder-working little Santo Niño is set in Spain. In Atocha, a suburb of Madrid, many men were imprisoned because of their faith. Prisoners were not fed by the jailers, so food was taken to them by their families. At one time the caliph issued an order that no one except children twelve years old and younger would be permitted to bring food to the prisoners. The women of the town appealed to Our Lady, begging her to help them find a way to feed the prisoners who had no young children in their family. Soon the other children came home from the prison with good news. The prisoners were being visited by a young boy. None of the children knew who he was, but the little water gourd he carried was never empty, and there was always

Santo Niño de Atocha

plenty of bread in his basket to feed all the hapless prisoners who had no children of their own to bring food. He came at night, slipping past the sleeping guards or smiling politely at those who were alert. Those who had asked the Virgin of Atocha for help began to suspect the identity of the little boy. As if in confirmation of the miracle, the shoes on the statue of the Child Jesus were constantly worn down and had to be replaced.

When the Spaniards came to the New World, they brought along the devotions of their native provinces. Those from Madrid naturally brought their devotion to Our Lady of Atocha. In 1540, silver mines were found in Mexico, and Spanish mineworkers migrated here.

In Plateros, a tiny village near the mines of Fresnillo, a church was built in honor of Santo Cristo de los Plateros, a miraculous crucifix, beginning in the late 1690s. A beautiful Spanish image of Our Lady and her Divine Child was placed on a side altar.

The original statue of Our Lady of Atocha held the Holy Child in her left arm. The child was made to be removable and at one time the original image was lost. A native artist made the replacement, and the new infant had Indian features. More of a doll than a sculpture, the image has a wig of human hair and his hands are oversized and roughly made. The parish priests began to take the Holy Child in procession during Christmas and the February feast of the Candelaria, the Virgin's Purification, to the parish church at nearby Fresnillo, dressing the Santo Niño in different clothing to emphasize seasonal festivities in the liturgical calendar.

By late colonial times, devotion to the Holy Child was rising and eclipsed the devotion to Our Lady of Atocha and also to the Santo Cristo of Plateros. In an inventory of 1816, the little image of the Christ Child is described as wearing a purple dress and holding a little globe of silver and a scepter. His dress was decorated with several silver Milagros, and artists had painted two retablos of thanksgiving from grateful clients. By 1838, a new inventory showed that the little image had been moved to a niche in the main altar. Still dressed as a child prince, he had gained a rosary and a belt and had twenty-nine outfits of clothing and thirty-two retablos (paintings on tin or wood given as ex-voto offerings).

Through the years, as Santo Niño's reputation as a miracle worker increased, the shrine in the sparsely populated and rugged mountainous area became a major place of pilgrimage. Santo Niño has received so many votive offerings that in 1883 a special building, the salon de retablos, was built to house them and serves as a museum at the shrine.

Just as his annual trips in pilgrimage to Fresnillo promoted his reputation as a wandering pilgrim, a novena in his honor written in 1848 contributed to his traditional patronages. The novena was written in completion of a *manda,* or vow, to praise the Holy Child in return for the author's recovery from a serious illness. Calixto Aguirre began his act of thanksgiving by traveling from Guanajuato to Plateros. Here, with the help of two men connected with the shrine, he transcribed the record of nine miracles from the retablos, using each as an inspirational theme for the day's prayers. The novena described the Holy Child with the attributes of a little wanderer rather than an infant king. The miracles described are in favor of prisoners and those unjustly accused, miners, immigrants, victims of poor economic conditions and crime, and the seriously ill. He has been called the patron of the *desamparados,* or "the neglected." Aguirre's novena had an enormous distribution in Mexico, New Mexico, and Central America, and Santo Niño's devotion spread rapidly.

The Shrine in Chimayo, New Mexico

In 1857, Severiano Medina from New Mexico made a pilgrimage to Fresnillo and returned with a small statue of the Holy Child. This statue was enshrined in a private chapel in Chimayo, near Santa Fe. There, history repeated itself and the devotion began to grow as it had in Fresnillo. At this shrine there is a *posito,* or well, where devotees come to take blessed dirt as a sacramental in honor of the Holy Child and as an aid to healing.

Some of the first American troops to see action in World War II were from the New Mexico National Guard. They fought bravely on Corregidor, with its underground tunnels and defenses. The Catholics remembered that the Santo Niño de Atocha had long been considered a patron of all who were trapped or imprisoned. Many of them made a vow that if they survived the war they would make a pilgrimage from Santa Fe to Chimayo at Thanksgiving. At the end of the war two thousand pilgrims, veterans of Corregidor, Bataan, and Japanese prison camps, and their families, walked the long and rough road from Santa Fe to Chimayo.

The wandering and wonder-working little Infant of Atocha visits the hearts of all with his tender love.

Blind Child Jesus
Niño Cieguito
Puebla, Mexico

At first glance the image of the Niño Cieguito seems surreal. Empty sockets with tears of blood stare from his tiny face. In one hand he holds a jeweled crucifix; in the other he holds a golden scepter to which two eyeballs are fixed. The child is sitting on a royal throne with a golden crown on his head amid a mass of blonde curls. He wears only a loincloth.

A sign at the church door tells visitors, "sacrilegious hands made this image blind." Some say the eyes of the image were gouged out during the persecution of the church in Mexico. Another pious legend tells of an earlier desecration.

When you cross the dim recess of the small church of the Capuchins to approach the lighted niche to the left of the main altar, the surreal image seems to change. The sweet and loving countenance of the Holy Child draws the viewer to tears of pity and sorrow for the sins of all humanity.

The story is told that in 1744 the statue was at a convent in Morelia. One summer night, a man broke into the convent church, vandalizing its sacred images. He stole the image of the Christ Child from its mother's arms and fled. The image began to cry, so the man stabbed it. The image continued to cry so the man tore out the valuable eyes made of gemstones and threw the damaged statue to the ground. When it was found, tears of blood were on its face. Later, the image was sent to the church of the Capuchins in Puebla.

Each Wednesday the church has a special healing Mass for the sick. El Niño Cieguito is known for his favors to the sick and terminally ill, especially seriously ill children. Little silver Milagros in the shape of hearts surround his niche in mute testimony of favors granted.

Thousands of the faithful come to venerate the little blind boy on his feast day, August 10. Day by day, devotees come in reparation for the outrage committed by the thief and the sins of humankind, which wound Our Lord. They pray to be liberated from eternal blindness of their souls.

The indulgenced prayer to the little blind Jesus reads: "O Holy Child Jesus, through the patience you had in suffering the outrages that a cruel and inhuman man did to your holy image, I pray you to grant me health. I ask through the intercession of our Holy Mother the Virgin Mary and in your honor I offer this Our Father and Hail Mary to make amends for my sins."

On April 30, the city of Puebla celebrates children, and the faithful visit and venerate the images of the Child Jesus that populate the many churches of the city. On that day, the altar of Niño Cieguito is covered with multicolored balloons, toys, and sweets. The entire city celebrates what Niño Cieguito's devotees know—that the Christ Child, too, was once a little boy.

Blind Child Jesus

Child of Good Luck
Santo Niño de las Suertes
Tacubaya, Mexico

The image of the Holy Child of Good Luck is a beautiful, yet graphic, reminder of our faith in the Resurrection. The tiny sleeping infant rests his head peacefully, using a human skull as a pillow.

The pious tradition of Santo Niño de las Suertes tells that in the early part of the nineteenth century, two missionary priests were crossing a large field in Tacubaya, a suburb of Mexico City, when they heard a baby crying piteously. There were no houses in the deserted area, so they began searching for the mysterious child.

At last, they found a beautiful little statue of the Holy Child, sleeping peacefully on a skull. As they picked it up, a spring, which still flows today, gushed forth from the ground. They took the statue to the archbishop, Francisco de Lizana Beaumont, and he received it with great devotion. On seeing the little image, he exclaimed, "How merciful is God. In such way He demonstrates to man how great is his grace. In his Divinity, he became man; by means of this grace he has overcome sin."

The saintly and mystic archbishop saw in the fortunate gift a reminder of the Resurrection. He wanted to give the statue to the Bernardine sisters at the convent of the Immaculate Conception in Tacubaya, but his *Cabildo* (advisors) convinced him to draw lots among all the convents of the city to choose its guardians.

At the drawing, the Bernardines won. The *Cabildo,* however, seeing that this was the poorest convent in the city, convinced him to draw a second time. Again, the Bernardines won. Telling him that the statue should go to a convent where the nuns didn't have

Child of Good Luck

to work so hard to make their living, the *Cabildo* convinced the holy archbishop to draw a third time.

This time, before he could shake the box, a paper with the name of the Bernardines written in gold letters appeared from the box. The archbishop understood that the image wanted to go to the poor convent, so he enriched the devotion with indulgences and gave the little treasure to the Bernardines. Full of gratitude, the sisters have kept the cult to this day with great zeal. They say that from the moment the image entered their convent happiness reigned there.

Today, the devotees of the Child of Good Fortune enter the little chapel attached to the convent, asking for favors and help in their daily lives and leaving presents of golden hearts and tiny toys for the Christ Child.

Holy Child of the Remedy
Santo Niño del Remedio
Madrid, Spain

A beautiful image of the Christ Child as a passion figure from the late sixteenth century remained unknown to the public until 1897. The owners at that time moved away from Spain and sold their possessions. Don Pedro Martin Mazarruela bought the statue for a hundred pesetas. He took it to his home on a busy street in the center of Madrid.

The Mazarruela family made a small chapel in their home in honor of the Holy Child. At the end of each day, Don Pedro, his wife, and their daughters gathered to pray before the little statue, asking the good God for all their needs.

Neighbors heard of the little chapel and also came to pray. Soon the entire neighborhood was talking about the many graces that seemed to be gained from prayers before the little image. Helped by a couple who had received several favors, Don Pedro enlarged the little chapel. More people began to visit and the devotion began to increase and to spread. One day even the Queen-Regent of Spain came incognito to visit the humble house of the Mazarruela family. Queen Christina came to pray to the Holy Child for the protection of her young son, Alfonso XIII, who had become king on the day of his birth.

Since the little statue had no name, Don Pedro and the chaplain of a nearby church decided to name it. They celebrated a Mass, asking God's help to choose between the names suggested: Child of Hope, of Pardon, of Consolation, and of the Remedy. The names were drawn twice, and both times the slip with the name of the Remedy came up. Since then, the image has been known as the Holy Child of the Remedy.

Soon, a confraternity was begun in honor of the Holy Child. A novena, a triduum, and a prayer were written and approved. Eventually, so many people came to venerate the image that a chapel of its own was needed. In 1917, the Child of the Remedy was carried in procession to an altar in a small church nearby. Since that time, numerous pious devotees have come to venerate the image of the Holy Child.

Through the years, the statue has been restored a number of times. In the eighteenth century, the head was cut in order to add crystal eyes, which were fashionable at the time. In the last restoration, the right foot had to be reconstructed because it had been worn away by the kisses of pious devotees. Today the feet are covered with silver shoes to prevent deterioration.

The little image of the Child of the Remedy has a sad expression and holds a cross in his hand. It is as if he contemplates his destiny. He does not run from the passion but steps boldly forward to redeem the world. Daily, people come to lay their troubles and open their hearts before the beloved little image of the Christ Child. On the thirteenth of each month, the pilgrims gather in numbers when the image is taken down and put in reach of all.

Holy Child of the Remedy

In 1993, Cardinal Angel Suquía assigned the Oratory of the Child of the Remedy to Catholic Action of Madrid, naming the chaplain of the group as rector of the church that contains the chapel to the Holy Child.

Incarnate Word
United States

Devotion to the Incarnate Word reached new heights as architects designed a place for a statue of the Christ Child on the exterior of many buildings throughout the American Southwest and Mexico. Following an inspiration and directives from Christ in prayer, Mother Jeanne de Matel founded the Incarnate Word and Blessed Sacrament sisters in Roanne and then moved later to Lyon, France, in 1625. In company with many other spiritual leaders of her time, Mother Jeanne de Matel (1596–1670) saw the mystery of the Incarnation personified in the Child Jesus. For her, devo-

Incarnate Word

tion to the Incarnate Word began with devotion to the Child Jesus, seeking to emulate the humility of the innocent Christ Child who emanates a pure and infinite love. By the late seventeenth century, statues of the Christ Child became very popular in other places of prayer.

This particular statue of the Incarnate Word shows him as a child of seven or eight, holding his right hand up in a gesture of blessing while his left hand holds an open book with the words Christ told to St. Peter: "If you love me come follow me."

This statue of the Child Jesus, recognized as the Incarnate

Word, became important in the apostolic work of the order in the United States and Mexico. At the request of the sisters, architects began to design a place on top of all buildings—and in the interior in many cases—in the convents and buildings where the Sisters of the Incarnate Word established communities throughout the late nineteenth and twentieth centuries.

Four sisters of the Incarnate Word left France, and, in 1852, they arrived in Texas bringing the devotion to the Incarnate Word with them. A year later they founded the first Incarnate Word convent and school in America at Brownsville, Texas. Hundreds of miles away in San Antonio the sisters established Incarnate Word Academy and in 1906 imported a marble statue of the Christ Child for their Romanesque chapel. Another beautiful statue of the Christ Child in the San Fernando cathedral commemorates the years of service given by the Sisters of Charity of the Incarnate Word who served at the cathedral school in the early twentieth century. As a Jubilee memorial to the Incarnate Word, students of the past century presented a statue of the Christ Child placed prominently in front of the Incarnate Word administration building.

Today, eleven congregations based on the spirituality of Venerable Jeanne de Matel serve in the United States, Mexico, Europe, Africa, and Central and South America. The statue continues to have a significant place in the buildings and houses where the sisters minister and live.

Child of the Blade
Niño de la Cuchilla
Zea, Venezuela

A tiny alabaster carving of the Holy Child known as the Niño de la Cuchilla (Child of the Blade) is venerated in Zea, in the state of Merida, Venezuela. The baby Jesus, only three and a half inches long, reclines on the slab of a grave. His head rests on his right

Child of the Blade

arm and he uses a human skull for a pillow. The globe of the world lies in front of him. The peaceful expression on the face of the child inspires our faith in Christ's Resurrection.

The complete history of the origin of the image is not known, and many pious legends have arisen about its arrival in Zea. However, according to careful research, the statue was originally in the possession of Clarist nuns whose cloister in Merida had been founded from Spain.

During the anticlerical regime of General Antonio Guzman White (1870–1877) in Venezuela, Catholic convents were closed and the religious expelled. Among those exclaustered were the Clarist nuns from Merida, who had in their possession the exquisite little alabaster sculpture. When they were besieged by soldiers who threatened to throw them in the street and carry the abbess to jail, they separated, carrying what they could of the monastery's possessions, intending to flee for asylum to Colombia. Two of the nuns walked and rode horses on their way to Bogota, to meet with others of their community. At Las Tapias de Bailadores, they were welcomed and sheltered overnight by a family named Hernandez who loaned them fresh horses and a servant to accompany them to the next stop. In gratitude for their help, the nuns gave the family the little sculpture of the Holy Child, which was originally from the Clarist convent in Spain.

The Hernandez family moved to Zea, and the Holy Child remained in the possession of their family and of their relatives for many years. At last it was given to some relatives named Vera who lived near the edge of the mountain in a part known as the Cuchilla, or blade, since here the crest of the mountain is as sharp as a knife. Too poor to afford even a small altar, the family placed the image on a little board in a small room, and began to honor and venerate it. Soon, miraculous favors were granted in answer to prayers, which called attention to the beautiful little image of the Christ Child.

In 1935, when the parish priest, Padre Ramón de J. Angulo, learned of the popular devotion, he determined to make a larger and more fitting place for the image. The sculpture was moved to an altar in the parish church where the people came to pray and to ask the Holy Child for favors. The blessings and favors multiplied. In 1949, with the cooperation of the parish priest and many of the town dignitaries, a beautiful new chapel was built in honor of the Santo Niño de la Cuchilla. Here, the little image was placed in a gold reliquary brought from Spain.

Each year on December 31, in the procession known as the "Lowering of the Holy Boy," the Holy Child is brought down to the town of Zea. Here the Santo Niño de la Cuchilla is celebrated in a weeklong joyful fiesta. Thousands come from all parts of the country to honor the Holy Child. On January 6, another colorful procession returns the little sculpture to its chapel in the mountains.

Infant Founder
Niño Fundador
Ada, Michigan

Of all the images and statues representing the infancy of Our Lord in the Carmel of Our Lady of Guadalupe, the one most cherished is the Infant Founder from Queretaro, Mexico. It was brought to Grand Rapids by Mother Mary Elias of the Blessed Sacrament (Mary Helen Thierry, 1879–1943).

The life-size image portrays the Infant Jesus in a sleeping pose. Made of wood composition and painted realistically, the statue is twenty-one inches long and has glass eyes, which are slightly open, with real eyelashes. The statue had been brought to the Carmel in Queretaro from Mexico City in 1803 and treasured there from generation to generation. While still in Queretaro, the paint on the face began to peel and the prioress wished to have it refinished. An artist consented to do the work, and when she came to the monastery, Mother Elias explained what she wanted done and gave her the statue. When the artist saw it, she asked Mother Elias again what needed to be done as the statue looked perfect to her. Receiving the image back, the prioress was amazed to see that the statue had repaired itself and was in beautiful condition, as it remains today.

The Carmel in Queretaro was founded from the Carmel in Mexico City in the nineteenth century. In 1867 it was closed and the nuns dispersed and exclaustered because of political unrest. In 1908 three sisters, including Sister Mary Elias, came from Mexico City to reestablish the foundation. By 1914, the sisters were again exclaustered because of the persecution of the church. Some of the sisters fled the country, dressed as laywomen.

As part of her disguise, Mother Elias carried the statue of the Infant Founder in her arms as if it were a real baby. The fact that her infant never cried was remarked on by one of the other passengers on the train. At that remark, according to the story, a tear fell from the eye of the statue and it made an audible little cry. The rest of the Queretaro community were reunited in Havana in 1915. From there, the sisters came to the United States, where they founded the Carmel of Our Lady of Guadalupe at the request of Bishop Henry Joseph Richter in Grand Rapids. Here, the little Mexican image of the Christ Child found his first home in the United States.

The Little Founder traveled to Buffalo with Mother Elias when the foundation was established there. At this Carmel, it was reported at times to have blushed and drooled. Eventually, both the Little Founder and Mother Elias returned to the Carmel in Grand Rapids (now moved to nearby Ada) where the valiant foundress passed to her eternal reward in 1943. The beloved little Infant remains, cherished by her spiritual daughters.

Most of the year, the Christ Child reigns in the oratory of the novitiate, watching over the novices. During the Christmas season until Epiphany, he is placed in a glass reliquary in the chapel where the public can see and venerate the little statue of the Christ Child. On the special days of clothing and profession, he is put on the altar of the oratory where the new novice or newly professed places her crown of roses at the end of the day. Every

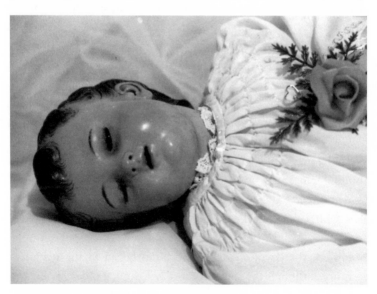

The Infant Founder

Christmas Eve, the nuns in their white mantles holding lighted candles follow the Mother Prioress, carrying the Holy Infant, in procession through the monastery. After the image is venerated, he is placed in a crib at the front of the choir and the chanting of Matins of the Divine Office for the feast of the Nativity begins.

For the nuns of Ada, the Infant Founder represents a precious heritage. He is a link with the past history of their sisters' love and heroism in coming to this country to save their religious vocation.

Divine Child
El Divino Niño
Bogota, Colombia

A happy little image of the Christ Child dressed in a pink tunic with his arms raised as if he waits for a hug represents probably the most popular devotion in Colombia today. Because of the many miracles attributed to prayers before the image, it vies in popularity with the ancient devotion to Señor de los Milagros. Thousands attend the Masses each weekend at the shrine in Bogota.

The devotion has spread worldwide since its inception in the first half of the twentieth century. After visiting the shrine in 1995, Mother Angelica, of Eternal Word Television, seemed to hear the image of El Divino Niño speaking to her, asking her to build a temple for him. The new shrine in Hanceville, Alabama, is dedicated to the Blessed Sacrament and Divino Niño.

Unlike many of the popular devotions surrounding images of the Christ Child whose historical origins are known only through tradition, the devotion to Divino Niño began in the twentieth century, although the statue itself may be much older.

The Salesian priest Father Giovanni Battista del Rizzo (1882– 1957) came to South America from Italy as a missionary, working first in Caracas, Venezuela, and then moving to Colombia in 1914. Father Rizzo had learned to love the Holy Child at the Italian shrine of Arenzano. In Colombia, this love and his trust was put to a test when he was sent out to solicit funds to help the Salesians build a new church. Embarrassed to be begging, he returned empty handed on the first day. When he was told to go again the following day, full of anguish he went to pray before the statue of Mary, Help of Christians. Raising his eyes, he saw the little Child Jesus, smiling with his arms outstretched as if to say "Take me with you. I want to accompany you." Then with all his soul, he pleaded that the Holy Child give him the courage to beg for the works of God. His prayers were answered. From that time, he became a great apostle of the Holy Child. He spoke of him, he worked for him, and he dedicated his life and all his energy to promote devotion to the infancy of Our Lord.

In 1935, Father Rizzo was transferred to a poor section in the south of Bogota called the Barrio Veinte de Julio, or twentieth of July. Convinced that it pleased God to honor Our Lord in his infancy, Father Juan—as he was called in Colombia—wanted to initiate the devotion in his new parish.

In a store in Bogota called Vaticano, owned by an Italian artist, Father Rizzo found a beautiful antique statue of the Christ Child. Smiling, with his little hands held out, the image was backed with a cross. In his usual joking manner, Father Rizzo said, "What! So little and already you want to crucify him? Take off that cross and I will take it." Father also asked the artist to place the words "Yo Reinaré" (I will reign) at the base of the statue. The artist made the requested change and Father Rizzo took the little image with him back to his poor barrio.

Here he began to preach to the people about the favors that the Christ Child does for those who have faith and who help the poor. Here, too, he built a small chapel in honor of the Divine Child. Soon, miracles and prodigies began to be reported. The devotion increased and began to spread. The people came first from neighboring barrios and then from the city. The government had to complete the road into the barrio because so many buses began to arrive, bringing people to pray to the Holy Child and to attend the Masses there.

Father John constantly preached a love for the poor and recommended that when asking the Holy Child for favors people should promise to give aid to those less fortunate. He also told people that when their prayers were answered they should tell others about the Holy Child. The cornerstone of the devotion, however, is faith. He often said, "Have faith and you will see miracles."

Father Rizzo took photographs of the little image and had copies made to distribute to all parts of the country in the form

El Divino Niño

of small *estampitas,* or holy cards. A large copy was made that the people began to carry in processions. Always Father John advised them to give thanks for all that the Holy Child had done for them and to tell others about his abundant mercy.

On Christmas of 1937 the first stone for a new church in honor of the Holy Child was blessed. The first church was a modest one, completed in 1942, and for forty years this church served an ever-increasing congregation. Finally, in 1989, the construction of a new and much larger church began and was completed in 1992.

The official name of the church and parish is El Niño Jesus, but the people all refer to it as El Divino Niño. In addition to the church, there is an annex and an open square. On Sundays, every hour on the hour, there is a Mass celebrated in two or three of the locations, and perhaps five thousand people attend each. The total number exceeds 100,000 people every Sunday.

Jesus, Doctor of the Sick
Jesus, Doctor de los Enfermos
Tepeaca, Mexico

A small statue known as Jesus, Doctor of the Sick, is honored in the city of Tepeaca, in Puebla, Mexico. Although it is a relatively new devotion, it is one of the most active in the southern part of a country full of popular devotions to the Holy Child. Comfort and health are given to those who go with faith and devotion to the little image of the Incarnate Word.

Once active persecution of the Catholic Church in Mexico ceased, many municipal governments began to remember the contribution the religious orders had made to the social services of the country. In 1942, a new municipal hospital opened, and the mayor of Tepeaca asked the Congregation of St. Joseph to staff it. An agreement was made, and the hospital opened with a big celebration, inaugurated by the new president of Mexico, Manuel Camacho, the governor of the state of Puebla, and the town's mayor.

Among the three sisters who served as nurses in the hospital was Sister Carmen Barrios Baez, who brought with her a beautiful image of the Child Jesus. Before coming to Tepeaca, Sister Carmen had worked in a hospital in Mexico City, where the little statue began to be called the Boy Doctor of the Sick. Sister Carmen would visit her patients, carrying the little image, and tell them that the doctors at the hospital would do their best for them but that they should pray to the best doctor of all, Jesus Christ.

In Tepeaca, Sister Carmen wanted the public to be able to venerate the image and put it in a small room of the hospital, which served as a chapel. The faithful who came to venerate it called it the Child of the Hospital. Soon, the devotion to the Holy Little Doctor began to grow and God conceded many signal favors to the devotees, especially the sick.

For a short while, Sister Carmen was transferred to Tehuacan, and took her beloved little Jesus with her. The faithful of Tepeaca pleaded for, and won, its return to the chapel in the hospital.

In 1961, the people began to celebrate an annual feast on April 30 at the parish church in honor of the Holy Child. In August of that year, due to their advanced age, the nuns withdrew from their work at the hospital, and the little image was taken to the home of Srta. Trinidad Flores Fuentes and put in her oratory where it was venerated until the death of Sister Carmen in July 1963.

After her death, according to Sister Carmen's wishes, the revered little image was transferred to a side altar of the parish church of San Francisco of Assisi.

As devotion to the Holy Little Doctor grew, his clients began to bring him new clothes as ex-voto offerings. A separate room

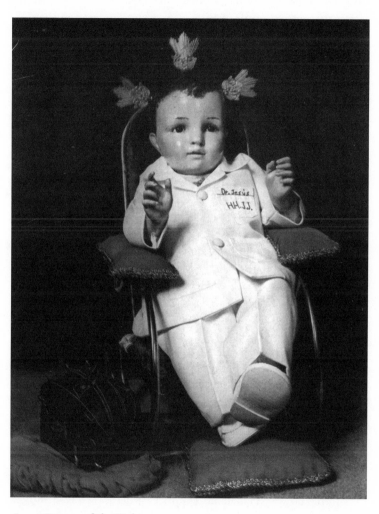

Jesus, Doctor of the Sick

near his chapel has a display of some of the many outfits he has been given as well as other votive offerings. The Holy Child is often dressed as a little doctor, complete with medical bag. At Christmas, the priest places him, dressed in one of his most beautiful outfits, on the main altar of the little church.

In 1991, a small chapel dedicated to the Holy Child was added to the church, and the remains of Sister Carmen were translated here. In a beautiful liturgical celebration, the Little Doctor was carried in procession to his new home. Here he is enshrined in a glass reliquary at the front of the chapel above eye level. Pilgrims walk up steps behind the altar and reach into the reliquary to touch the cape of the little image. Archbishop Rosendo Huesca y Pacheco solemnly blessed the chapel from which the Holy Child Jesus, Doctor of the Sick, continues to radiate love, trust, comfort, and blessings.

Infant of Bethlehem
Little Sisters of Jesus
Worldwide

The Little Sisters of Jesus place simple little statues of the Infant Jesus in hay-filled cribs at their fraternities throughout the world at Christmas. The babe, whose features incorporate and reflect all the cultures of humankind, holds his tiny hands up in a gesture that invites the viewer to reach toward it in a kind of aching longing to hold the humble Infant Jesus.

Little Sister Magdeleine (Hutin) of Jesus (1898–1989), a French woman, traveled to Algiers and founded the Little Sisters of Jesus in 1939, based on the ideals of Blessed Charles de Foucauld. Charles had conceived of a new kind of contemplative life where a fraternity of men and women would live prayerfully and simply among their Muslim neighbors and would proclaim the gospel—not with their words but with their actions.

At first, Magdeleine believed the mission of the Little Sisters was exclusively in relation to the Muslims of North Africa, and it was here that the congregation began and flourished. Gradually, however, she envisioned a universal mission, and, by the time of her death, there were Little Sisters in over sixty countries throughout the world made up of women from all races and nationalities. Committed to contemplative prayer, they joined in the life and culture of their neighbors, crying the Gospel with their lives rather than with their words.

> To cry the Gospel by your whole life means trying to live as Jesus lived, with the Gospel to give you light. It means living His self-surrender as a tiny child in the crib in Bethlehem, His poverty and His very ordinary life in Nazareth, both His contemplative life and His active charity on the roads during his public ministry, His surrender to God, His Father, in the pain of the passion and of the crucifixion. It means trying to love as He loved, living in the spirit of the beatitudes: in poverty, in gentleness, in a thirst for justice, being merciful, being pure of heart, and rejoicing when you suffer persecution out of love for Christ. (Little Sister Magdeleine of Jesus)

Magdeleine experienced intense visions inspired by her meditations on the Infant Jesus. Seeing the humility, weakness, and vulnerability of the Christ Child, she felt this divine baby should also be the inspiration and model for those who bore witness to divine love among the poorest and most powerless of the world. She said:

> I would like to pass on to my little sisters the important ideal of a holiness which is human. I want them to fix their eyes and

their heart on the life of Jesus which was so simple, so that they can get the taste for the extraordinary out of their minds forever, unless, of course, it's a taste for the extraordinarily simple. Then, onto this humanity, we must graft divine love, a love without measure.

The first statues of the Infant Jesus were made by members of the fraternity after World War II in Aix-en-Provence in the south of France. A Mr. Hartman, a French potter living nearby, taught some of the sisters how to make molds and form the clay. Since then a variety of images have been made by the sisters in several of the fraternities throughout the world. In the United States, the sisters of the fraternity in Gallitzin, Pennsylvania, continue to make and to sell the figurines. There is an expression of happiness and love on the face of each of the little statues of the Christ Child made by the Little Sisters of Jesus.

Infant Jesus of Good Health
Santo Niño de Buen Salud
Morelia, Mexico

In 1939, Rosa Calderon, a young girl in Morelia, received a small wood carving of the Child Jesus as a gift from her godmother for her First Communion. About eleven inches tall with natural coloring and glass eyes shadowed by dark eyelashes, the Christ Child held his left hand up in blessing.

Today, known as the Infant Jesus of Good Health, he is dressed royally. His right hand holds a golden scepter. He is crowned with a precious gold crown and his robe is trimmed with ermine. Although shown with the attributes of royalty and power, his sweet, childish countenance inspires the viewer with thoughts of love and protection.

Rosa and her family began to venerate the image, and it

*Infant Jesus
of Good Health*

seemed as if God granted special favors whenever he was peti-
tioned in their small family oratory. Rosa, an excellent seamstress,
dressed the infant in beautiful clothing and showered it with
affection. Later, friends and neighbors began to come to the
Calderon home to pray before the image, and they, too, were
granted graces of physical and spiritual healing. The fame of the
little Christ Child began to spread, and favors obtained through
his intercession became known. Soon, the archbishop of Morelia
approved private devotion to the little image.

The little statue was taken to the church of the Capuchins in
1942 and public veneration was approved. In 1957, it was transferred in solemn procession to the church of the ancient convent
of Our Lady of Mt. Carmel. With pastoral zeal, Archbishop Luis
M. Altamirano y Bulnes began to promote the devotion. In 1958,
the cornerstone was laid for a new church, built in honor of the
Infant of Good Health. The parish church of the Infant of Good

Health was consecrated in 1963. Here, the statue of the Holy Infant is enshrined in a niche in the upper part of the frontal wall. A replica of the original miraculous statue is used as a pilgrim statue, to be carried out in procession and to encourage the devotion in other places.

April 21 is the feast day of the Santo Niño. On the last Sunday in April, thousands of pilgrims from Mexico and the United States travel to Morelia to celebrate. Nine days prior to the celebration, a novena is held in the Morelia cathedral. On the last day of the novena, in the evening, there is a three-mile parade from the cathedral to the Holy Infant Church with the statue carried on a decorated float.

The Missionaries of the Infant Jesus of Good Health, founded by Rosa Calderon, known as Mother Lupita, promote the devotion and carry Jesus' message of salvation to all peoples by means of the pilgrim statue. They also serve by their work in childcare and pastoral service. In the United States the devotion is promoted, and there is a replica of the statue of the Infant of Good Health at Our Lady of the Holy Spirit Center in Norwood, Ohio.

Infant Jesus
Viveknagar (Bangalore), India

The beloved images of the Holy Child are enshrined in many beautiful and elaborate shrines and churches throughout the world. The first shrine for one of them, however, was in a tent with only an old wooden door for an altar. Here, for eight years, people came to worship God and to venerate an image of the Infant of Prague. Today, the shrine is a magnificent new church in a thriving parish of about twenty-five thousand Catholics.

In 1969, Sacred Heart parish had grown so large that it

needed to be split. In addition, many of the parishioners were from outlying towns and found it difficult to get to Sacred Heart. The pastor began to look for a piece of property to buy for a new parish but was unsuccessful in finding one. A pious parishioner with a deep devotion to the Infant Jesus suggested that he make a novena to the Infant of Prague for success. The pastor made the novena, adding the promise that if a suitable and affordable plot were found, he would build a shrine in honor of the Infant Jesus. By the end of the year, a plot was obtained at a windfall price. The agricultural acreage was in Viveknagar in the center of a rose field, which produced about three thousand roses per day. It was a beautiful place for a new church.

In 1971, the foundation stone was laid for the Church of the

Infant Jesus

Infant Jesus. The new pastor held Sunday Mass in the open rose field. The first tent covered only the altar, but later some old tents were acquired to shelter the congregation and an image of the Infant of Prague. The tent church survived the vagaries of weather for eight years, and year after year the congregation increased in number and in fervor. An old shed on the property was modified for a presbytery, and soon religious sisters and volunteers came to open a dispensary to serve the poor of the area and to teach catechism.

Even before a permanent church was built, the parish began to celebrate a feast of the Holy Child each January 14. Through the years, the celebration has grown steadily, as it seems the Holy Child has blessed many people by letting fall a shower of favors and graces in answer to their prayers. A museum at the shrine holds thousands of votive offerings, in mute testimony of gratitude for favors and blessings.

The image of the Infant Jesus at Viveknagar has a large wardrobe and his clothing is changed daily. Devotees often place garlands of flowers around his neck and pray with lighted candles in their hands.

During the feast-day celebrations, a large statue of the infant is taken in a decorated car to all the small towns in the area. Along the way, Christians and non-Christians alike come to see the procession pass. The people throw salt and flower petals at the image as it goes by. Many pious devotees walk along in the procession, praying and singing.

Today the shrine compound includes a school and a home for the aged as well as other social services. In addition to the throngs of pious pilgrims who flock to the shrine, especially on Thursday when the novena is prayed, non-Catholics also come.

Here in Viveknagar, the Christ Child is no longer enshrined in a tent. He is enshrined in a magnificent church of stone, but, more importantly, he is enshrined in the hearts of thousands of the faithful who know the truth of his divine promise: "The more you honor Me, the more I will bless you."

Holy Child of the Doves
El Niño de las Palomitas
Tacoaleche, Mexico

One of the most unusual temples of the Holy Child is a converted airplane hangar in Tacoaleche, Guadalupe Zacatecas. Here, visitors greet a happy little image of the Christ Child known as the Child of the Doves.

Although the devotion to the Child of the Doves originated in 1944 in Mexico City, devotion in Zacatecas only began in the early 1970s. Originally begun and promoted by the Spanish Carmelite Father Clemente of St. Joseph Murúa (1879–1974), the devotion spread to the state of Zacatecas through a healing miracle worked in favor of a member of a ranching family there.

In gratitude for a family member's cure and return to health, in 1973 a family at the Rancho San Carlos in Zacatecas had a replica of the original statue made for their home. This image, the work of the sculptor Miguel Juárez, has a third dove near his left foot. A beautiful work of art, the little image of Jesus seems to radiate peace and faith. From the small family oratory, the devotion began to spread, and many favors were reported. The image gained a reputation as a miracle worker, a thaumaturge. By 1976, so many people were coming to the little family oratory that the archbishop of Zacatecas authorized the construction of a new chapel. In 1989, the archbishop closed the chapel and ordered the image translated to a temporary shrine closer to the highway. This shrine is in a hanger of an old airport at Tacoaleche, near the town of Palomitas. Eventually, a new and permanent church will be built.

Today, the shrine is a popular place of pilgrimage, especially from the states of central Mexico, although the devotion has crossed the border to the United States with the wave of Mexican Catholic immigrants. On weekends, the cement parking area is filled with buses and private cars of tourists and devotees. By 1990, the shrine attracted a thousand visitors and by 2004 over fourteen thousand visitors came to venerate the little image.

Holy Child of the Doves

The original image of the Child of the Doves was made in Spain and given as a gift to Father Clemente who brought it with him to Mexico. The Child Jesus is standing, holding two doves. The devotion was approved by the archbishop of Mexico in 1944, and in 1945 the image was placed on a special altar in the ancient Church of Our Lady of Carmel, where the Carmelites began their apostolic labors on the American continent in 1585.

The Child of the Doves has light brown hair, large brown eyes, and a mouth open in a smile of welcome. The white doves he holds symbolize not only purity, innocence, and simplicity but also the souls of those who want to live in Jesus' love. The rector of the shrine, Father Gustavo Guijarro Montes, explains that the image represents Jesus who lives in us and who, just as he has done for the past two thousand years, calls the multitudes. Much of the devotion to the Holy Child emphasizes biblical references, and study bibles are prominent among the items sold in the shrine gift shop. Even the modernistic emblem of the shrine is a lesson. A cross and a circle are symbolic of Christ as true man and true God. At the base of the cross is an arrow with a dove, symbolic of the person who revolves around Jesus, making Jesus the center of his life.

The prayer to the Child of the Doves recognizes Christ as true man and true God and asks for his kindness and mercy to those who come to him in humility and with confidence. At Tacoaleche, hearts are drawn as if to a magnet by the graceful, childish image of the Holy Child of the Doves. In the same manner that the multitudes followed Jesus, pilgrims come to a humble shrine near a poor town to receive the Word and to see his miracles.

VII

Snapshots

A Photo Gallery of the Infant

Thousands of other famous and not-so-famous images of the Christ Child exist throughout the world in churches, religious houses, and private homes. Each has its own story, although the true history of many remains buried in the mists of time. Representations of Our Lord have been venerated and specially honored by the saints, in many religious orders, and by those who love the Holy Child and are loved by him in return.

Child Jesus of Teresa of Avila

Saint Teresa of Avila (1515–1582), the Spanish mystic and reformer of Carmel, was deeply devoted to the infancy of Our Lord. As she traveled throughout Spain, establishing seventeen new foundations of the reformed Discalced Carmelite nuns, she brought with her statues of the Christ Child, leaving one as a gift for each new foundation. A number of these images are still in existence today. Teresa was canonized in 1622 and acclaimed a Doctor of the Church in 1970. A pious story tells that once Teresa was interrupted by a little boy while she was at prayer. The child asked, "Who are you?" She answered, "I am Teresa of Jesus, and who are you?" The child replied, "I am Jesus of Teresa" and disappeared.

*Child Jesus
of Teresa of Avila*

Infant Jesus of Vincent Pallotti

Saint Vincent Pallotti (1795–1850), founder of the Society of the Catholic Apostolate (the Pallottines) and precursor of Catholic Action, had a deep devotion to the Christ Child. In order to encourage this devotion, he commissioned a Roman sculptor to make a statue of the Holy Bambino. The beautiful image is venerated in the church of San Salvatore in Onda in Rome. A copy of this statue is in the Infant Jesus Shrine in North Tonawanda, New York, dedicated in 1979.

The statue depicts the Christ Child in a natural and simple

pose, seated on a small pillowed chair. The babe is dressed in swaddling clothes, and his chubby baby arms are held out in a pose suggesting that he is waiting to hug those who come to venerate him. The right foot of the original statue is covered with a protective plate because of the Roman custom of kissing the foot of the image.

There are many beautiful examples of eighteenth-century *presépios*, or manger scenes, in Rome. In the nineteenth century,

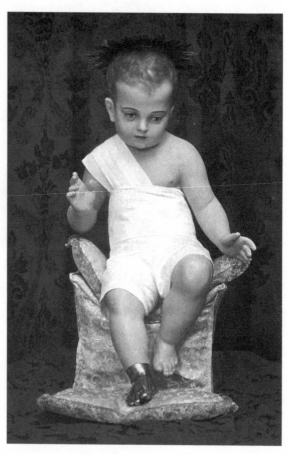

Infant Jesus of Vincent Pallotti

the custom of displaying the *presépio* spread to all levels of society with the production of inexpensive figures in terracotta. Some were built in church porches or balconies with natural scenery and the sky as a background. Even today, people visit these lovely works of art throughout Rome during the Christmas season. The most famous of all is the giant nativity scene built in St. Peter's Square every year during Advent since 1982 at the request of Pope John Paul II. The figures, from the eighteenth century and larger than life, were made for Saint Vincent Pallotti and donated by the Pallottine Fathers to the pope. The *presépio* is opened on Christmas Eve, and one of the first visitors is the pope himself. It is taken down after the season and the statues are carefully stored for the coming Christmas.

El Doctorcito of Rose of Lima

Isabel Flores de Oliva, better known as Saint Rose of Lima (1586–1617) was a Dominican tertiary and mystic and is the first can-

El Doctorcito of Rose of Lima

onized saint of the New World. Although her parents wanted her to marry, she lived as a recluse in a small house behind her parents' home, which she and her brother built. She spent her life in penance and service to the poor. Today, her relics rest at the Church and Shrine of Saint Rose in Lima, Peru. Here, too, one can find the celebrated little Doctorcito, a little Spanish statue of the Holy Child that Rose venerated as her helper when she attended the sick. Isabel's father had given her the statue when she was a child. She named the little image "The Doctor," and popular devotion to the image began to flourish.

Bambino of Blessed Lodovico Pavoni

Blessed Lodovico Pavoni (1784–1849) was an Italian priest from Brescia who spent his life in service to the young, using the means of positive education. In 1825, he founded a religious congregation of priests and brothers to run the educational and industrial activities that grew out of his institution. Pavoni concentrated on the personal and social formation of the young with a positive and preventative approach. The first trade taught in his oratory was book publishing. In 1823 he set up the Publishing House of the Institute of St. Barnabas, the precursor of today's Ancora Press. He also began teaching other trades such as carpentry, silversmithing, and tool and dye making. Long before the publication of the encyclical *Rerum novarum,* Pavoni grasped the religious significance of social justice and set an example by his own actions. Members of his religious congregation still publish books, and, in Rome, they staff the Ancora bookstore outside St. Peter's Square.

Infant Jesus of Venerable Celeste Crostarosa

The mystic and foundress of the Redemptoristine nuns, Venerable Celeste Crostarosa (1696–1755), dressed this image of the

Bambino of Blessed Lodovico Pavoni

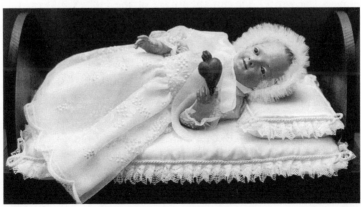

Infant Jesus of Venerable Celeste Crostarosa

Infant Jesus, which is treasured today in her Italian monastery at Foggia. The infant holds his heart in his left hand as a symbol of God's love in taking on our human nature. The redemptive spirituality of Celeste's order concentrates heavily on the human life of Jesus and the redemption he obtained for the world through his life, death, and resurrection. Celeste reminds us: "The humiliations of Jesus' humanity are the keys to the divine treasures of the living God."

Child Jesus Images of Thérèse of Lisieux

Saint Thérèse Martin (1873–1897) was given the religious name "of the Child Jesus" and had a lifelong devotion to the Holy Child. In her autobiography, *Story of a Soul,* she writes that on entering the cloister, "the first thing that struck my eye was the statue of the Little Jesus smiling at me from the midst of flowers and light." This devotion lasted until her death. The Christmas before she died, she wrote a beautiful poem illustrating the paradox of the Incarnation. The Child Jesus is also the subject of two other poems and two of her Christmas plays as well as some of the prayers she wrote. She put the image of the Holy Child on the coat of arms she designed for herself. She particularly treasured some holy cards of the child that had been given to her by friends. The cult of the Child Jesus thrived at the Carmel of Lisieux, France, and there were many images of the Christ Child that Thérèse would have seen daily. A copy of the Little King of Beaune overlooked the choir. As in most Carmels, there was a copy of the Infant of Prague statue. Thérèse loved to decorate with flowers a small altar to the Holy Child in the cloister. One particular treasure of the convent today is a small wax sculpture of the Christ Child, which is dressed in cloth from the dress she wore on the day she took the habit. The Alençon lace on the

Child Jesus Image of Thérèse of Lisieux

image was made by her mother and its hair is from the saint, cut when she was young. Thérèse used her artistic talent and painted at least two pictures of the Child Jesus and decorated a number of cards by adding painted flowers to them.

Infant Jesus of Antonie Werr

Antonie Werr (1813–1868), the foundress of the (Franciscan) Servants of the Holy Child Jesus at Oberzell, Germany, recognized that not only did God become a man but, in doing so, he first became a child. In his humble birth, she saw the creator of all things assume the form of a slave. This mystery of faith so affected her that she chose it as the name of her foundation. For Antonie, the Gospel of the Incarnation was the pillar of her spirituality, and she told her sisters, "since no one was ever more humble than the Child Jesus, . . . if you wish to please the divine Child, like him you must love humility and renounce all pride and arrogance."

An image of the Christ Child in swaddling clothes is venerated by Antonie's spiritual daughters throughout the world. Tradition holds that the original picture, treasured by the sisters at the motherhouse in Oberzell, was received in a unique way. On Christmas Eve of 1855, the sisters were praying to the Holy Child when a mysterious woman dressed in black appeared and presented the picture to the mother foundress.

Poor Child Jesus of Clara Fey

At the age of eleven, young Clara Fey (1815–1894) had a prophetic dream. She was walking along a street near her home in Aix-la-Chapelle; she stopped to look at an old building, a former church and convent that had been used as a warehouse since the days of Napoleon. Suddenly she noticed a little boy, poorly dressed, looking as if he wanted alms. As she reached for a coin, the little boy said pleadingly, "I have many poor little brothers and sisters." When Clara asked the child where he lived, he smiled and said "I am the poor Child Jesus." Immediately the child disappeared and Clara awoke. From that time, she saw all poor and neglected children as brothers and sisters of the Poor Child Jesus. Nineteenth-century Europe was recovering from the horrors of the French Revolution; workers were needed to bring the spirit of religion back to the people. The Industrial Revolution with all its positive points also brought about abuses in child labor and child neglect. Seeing the wretched conditions of many poor children of the city who were working long hours in factories and younger ones left alone at home to wander the streets, Clara and three like-minded women banded together in 1844 to educate and care for these children. The constitutions of the Congregation of the Poor Child Jesus, which they founded, aimed at promoting a simplicity of character and joyful spirit in imitation of the Child Jesus, born in poverty. A painting by one of the sisters—Sister Mary Amabilis, of Simpelveld, Holland—shows the Venerable Clara leading little children to the Poor Child Jesus in the manger at Bethlehem.

Poor Child Jesus of Clara Fey

The Little Imperator of Lorenzo Salvi

Blessed Lorenzo Salvi (1782–1856) was a Passionist missionary and apostle of the Infant Jesus in Viterbo, Italy. In 1812, he saw a vision of the Child Jesus and was cured from a serious illness. From that time, he became a dedicated apostle of the devotion to the Infant Christ. He worked several marvels through the image he always carried with him, which he called my Little Imperator. This image, a painting by Antonio Canova, had been given to Blessed Lorenzo. To his four Passionist vows, he added a personal fifth one: to foster devotion to the Infant Jesus. He wrote several books including *The Soul in Love with the Infant Jesus*. He sculpted an image of the Holy Child, which he had copied for distribution, and made and distributed small printed images of the Holy Child. Through his life he witnessed to the incarnation of God in the infancy of Jesus.

Holy Child of the Smile

Holy Child of the Smile (Santo Niño de la Sonrisa)

This smiling little image of the Christ Child is venerated at the church of San Jose in Puebla, Mexico. The sculpture is dressed and usually displayed seated in a little chair, as is customary throughout the country, on February 2, the feast of the Presentation (*candelaria*). The depiction of the holy little boy is surrounded by toys, favorite votive offerings from grateful clients.

El Niño Jesús de Belén

A tiny image of the Holy Child, barely as long as an adult's thumb, is venerated in Sonsonate, El Salvador, under the title El Niño Jesús de Belén. Beautifully ornamented with marine animals, it washed ashore in 1945.

The young son of a poor fisherman was walking along the beach of la Playa de las Flores in the area of Sonsonate, Acajutla, one day, when he spied what looked like an unusual seashell clinging to a rock. When he picked it up, he realized that it was a tiny china image of the Christ Child that had been meticulously covered with nacre, the hard pearly layer of certain sea shells. The sea animals had formed a small cradle and covered the little body in swaddling clothes of a porous type of coral, completing it with a cap over the tiny head. The little face with its pink cheeks and the arms were left uncovered and had not been damaged by the statue's long bath in the ocean.

Joyously, the boy carried his unique find home to Izalco, where the family placed it in their Christmas crib. At this time, some Carmelite sisters of Saint Joseph, including their superior general Mother Paula of the Divine Savior, were visiting the little town, and, since it was near Christmas, they went to visit the dif-

El Niño Jesús de Belén

ferent manger scenes, known as *nacimientos,* traditionally set up as attractive displays in each home.

When they arrived at the fisherman's home, at first they could not see where the Christ Child was placed in the *nacimiento* because it was so small. When it was pointed out to them they were amazed and delighted and begged to be allowed to take it back to their school at San Tecla. There, the Holy Infant seemed to delight in answering the prayers of those who came to him in simple faith. After a brief study, Bishop Chavez y Gonzalez approved the devotion.

Santo Niño de Petare

One of the oldest images in the church of the Sweet Name of Jesús in Petare, Venezuela, is the Santo Niño, a unique sculpture

Santo Niño de Petare

of the Holy Child cast in metal. The statue first appears in an inventory of the church in 1650, but probably arrived in Petare during the first years of the city's founding thirty years earlier. The statue represents the boy Jesus at about the age of four years in a standing position with open arms. In his left hand he holds a cross, and his right hand is raised in blessing. Made of lead, the statue is nearly twenty-six inches tall. Traditionally, the statue is always dressed in a robe of seventeenth-century design when it is exhibited, although the entire figure is completely finished. The majority of statues made in this period were of wood. The Petare image is molded of lead, and a few examples of this type are still found in cloistered convents in Andalusia, where some statues of this type were produced. During the first decades of the seventeenth century, a number of these statues were brought from the workshops of Seville in Spain to America. One series of images of the young savior, made for export to the colonies, was created by the Spanish sculptor Juan Martinez Montañez, who influenced many other Spanish artists of his day. Taking into account the year that this image appeared in Petare and its similarity in style to other images of the *montañesina* school, it is possible that the Petare statue is one of the series of images of the Holy Child brought to the colonies in the first decades of the seventeenth century.

Infant of Prague
Carmel of St. Teresa, Alhambra, California

The Infant of Prague is venerated in the chapel, which is dedicated to him, as well as in the cloister of the Carmelite Nuns in Alhambra, California. These nuns came to Los Angeles in 1913,

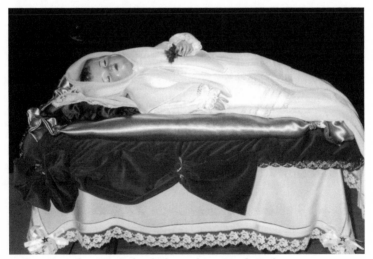

Infant Founder, Carmels of Alexandria, South Dakota, and Buffalo, New York

and eventually they acquired enough money to build the monastery in what was then a rural section of Alhambra. Unfortunately, there was not enough money to build a chapel. The archbishop suggested they move in at once and build the chapel later. This was a source of great sorrow to the foundress, Mother Baptista, who greatly desired to build a house for Our Lord. She prayed to the infant for help, and shortly afterward a wealthy couple went to the archbishop and offered funds for a memorial to the lady's parents. At his suggestion they dedicated the funds to build a chapel for the nuns. The chapel was consecrated in 1926 and the image is still venerated there.

Infant Founder
Carmels of Alexandria, South Dakota, and Buffalo, New York

Copies of the miraculous Infant Jesus Founder image brought by Mother Mary Elias of the Blessed Sacrament, OCD, from Queretaro, Mexico, to the United States are in the Carmelite Monastery of Our Mother of Mercy and St. Joseph in Alexandria, South Dakota, and in the Carmelite Monastery of St. Therese in Buffalo, New York (see p. 138 for the story of the original of this image). In Buffalo, where the original was once venerated, the copy is carried in solemn procession through the monastery on Christmas Eve during the procession before Midnight Mass as an act of petitioning his blessing on every corner of the monastery.

In the Carmel in South Dakota the copy of Mother Elias's miraculous image is also taken in procession on Christmas Eve. During solemn professions, he is placed on the altar in the choir. Recently, the Child Jesus seemed to grant a special favor to one of the young sisters making her solemn profession. The ceremony was set for a hot August day in 2003. The family was in the process of relocating, so the sister's family drove up from Texas while her father flew in from another state. Unfortunately, he was stranded in the Detroit airport on August 14 because of a power outage and could not make it in time for the ceremony on the following morning. The boutonniere he was to wear was placed instead in the hands of the statue of the Infant Jesus who would later receive the young sister's written vows. The ceremony was beautiful, but the heat was so extreme that the crown of the newly professed and her mother's corsage wilted. When her father arrived that afternoon, the boutonniere showed no sign of wilting; the Infant had kept it fresh to welcome him.

Images of the Carmel of Alexandria, South Dakota

The Carmel in South Dakota has a number of other images of the Holy Child. One, known as the Little Founder, was given to the sisters from Buffalo who came to make the new foundation. It is an image of the Little King of Prague, dressed as a Carmelite friar. Another image is known as the Pilgrim (El Peregrinito). It is an exact replica of a statue kept in the Carmel of Valladolid, Spain, which was founded by Teresa of Avila in 1569. The saint had given the original to the first nun professed in Valladolid, Sr. Anne of St. Joseph. This copy was given to the nuns in Pittsford, New York, in 1969 in gratitude for their many charities. The statue was sent to South Dakota when the monastery in New York closed.

Manuelitos of Cuzco, Peru

A highlight of the Christmas season in Cuzco is the Santurantikuy, the Andean Christmas market. Traditional *nacimientos* (manger scenes) are set up in churches and homes, and the people flock to the market on December 24 to purchases new images for their elaborate displays. The favorites, of course, are the

Image of the Carmel of Alexandria, South Dakota

images of the Christ Child, known as Manuelitos, a familiar use of the name Emmanuel. For centuries, artists in the Cuzco area have sculpted images of the Holy Child, passing down the secrets of their art, generation to generation, through the families noted for this work. The homes of the barrio San Blas are also work-shops and stores dedicated to the Holy Child. The little sculp-tures are made of maguey covered with a unique paste that imparts a lifelike blush to the skin. The statues are fitted with realistic glass eyes and teeth made from the tubular base of condor feathers. Children's hair is rolled in a tube of straw and boiled in lemon, then added to the sculptures. The divine infant is modeled in different positions: asleep in his crib, catching a wisp of air with tiny, chubby hands, or in one of the poses well known in the area.

Perhaps the most famous of the Manuelitos of Cuzco is El Niño de la Espina, the Child of the Thorn, but there are many other traditional devotions associated with named images of the Christ Child. El Niño Saltarin, or the Jumping Boy, celebrates the miracle of a statue that came to life and was seen playing Plik Plak (hopscotch) with the angels in a convent of Lima. When he realized he had been seen, he froze with his foot in the air. The Divine Bread Thief, or the Niño Robapanes, represents the Christ Child whose legend tells that he took bread from a baker in Oropesa and gave it to the poor. In Ayacucho, he is known as the Boy of the Sling, or Niño Honderito. In times of drought, the farmers bring him candies and sponge cakes and put a woven slingshot full of stones in his hands, asking him to shoot the clouds to bring rain. In the Manuelitos of Cuzco, the love and devotion of the Peruvian people to the Christ Child can be seen in the faces of the many statues typical of the area.

Santo Niño de la Gracia

This image of the Christ Child is by an anonymous sculptor of the eighteenth century. It is found in a chapel of the Pontifical Basilica of San Miguel in Madrid, Spain. The Hermandad del Santísimo Cristo de la Fe y del Perdón (Confraternity of the Holy Christ of Faith and Forgiveness) is the custodian of the image and its attendant devotion.

*Santo Niño
de la Gracia*

Infant Jesus Shrine of Benin City, Nigeria

After the death of her daughter in the late 1990s, a member of St. Joseph parish in Benin City came upon a booklet with the story of the Infant of Prague. Touched by the tender story, she proposed starting the devotion at the church in Benin City. The Jesuits at the church liked the idea because the devotion centered on three things they felt were important for the parish: (1) Jesus. There were already societies to some of the saints, but this devotion centered on Jesus in his helpless, dependent phase. His weakness emanates God's power. (2) Children and youth. A children's choir was begun, which sings at the Vigil Mass; there are liturgical dancers who are very young children, and there is a youth branch

Infant Jesus Shrine in Africa

of the Infant Jesus group, which sponsors children- and youth-related activities. (3) Poor. Right from its inception the members of the Infant Jesus society were radically involved in founding a soup kitchen to cook for and to feed the destitute of the area. Although the cooking started in the backyard of the parish house, it has now become more permanently lodged in Joseph House, a parish house for various social ministries.

Santo Niño Mueve Corazones

Santo Niño Mueve Corazones, "the Holy Child moves hearts," is a popular saying in Mexico. Numerous images throughout the country reflect this association of the Christ Child and his ability to touch the human heart. One statue known as Santo Niño Mueve Corazones is found in the church Nuestra Señora del Carmen in Cuauhtemoc, a part of the historical district of Mexico

Santo Niño Mueve Corazones

City. The statue shows Jesus holding a basket of hearts in his left hand and presenting a heart to the viewer with his right hand. Small pictures of this statue were photographically reproduced in postcard size, were colored by hand, and were distributed widely during the 1960s. A popular Mexican print shows the young Jesus standing in a field holding three hearts and is also called Santo Niño Mueve Corazones. In the painting of the Holy Mother of the Light, the Christ Child holds a heart that he enflames with love while an angel standing at the feet of the virgin presents him with a basket of hearts.

Child of the Kiss

A statue of the Incarnate Word stands at the main entrance to the Holy Child church in Tijeras, New Mexico. As the people enter, after blessing themselves with holy water, they then kiss the statue or touch it tenderly and reverently as they pass by. The ladies of the Altar Rosary society who clean the church say that the little Jesus usually has lipstick on his cheeks or forehead. Holy Child parish is in the Archdiocese of Santa Fe, about ten miles east of Albuquerque. Originally a mission church, it was established as a parish in 1964 and has grown to about fifteen hundred families. No records have been located as to the origin of the statue, which has been in place since the church was built.

Palaboy (Wandering Holy Child)

In the Philippines, a little vagabond image known as Santo Niñong Gala, or the Palaboy, is a popular image of the Christ Child. The word *palaboy* is a Tagalog word meaning "homeless." The image carries a walking stick, sometimes shaped like a cross, and one hand is raised in blessing. Dressed like a young Filipino boy, he wears shorts, a *sando* (sleeveless undershirt), and a little straw hat. Sometimes he carries a bundle tied to a stick. He goes about shoeless or in sandals. This image of the Christ Child is found not in any particular church but rather in the homes of the people. The image was created and sculpted as a result of Filipino fondness for the Santo Niño. Pious legends tell that he roams about, particularly in rural areas, visiting farmers and fishermen

Child of the Kiss

Palaboy

and testing the charity of the people he encounters. How did he come by his ambulatory reputation? No one knows exactly but possibly from the story of the "walking" of the Santo Niño de Cebu, which was at one time transferred to Manilla and "walked" back to Cebu until it was permanently enshrined there.

Hummelwerkes Child Jesus
Siessen, Germany

Possibly no other artist has ever so successfully portrayed the captivating innocence of early childhood as did Sister Berta Innocentia Hummel, a German Franciscan nun. In the 1930s, Sister Innocentia's art helped support her convent and became the basis for figurines that remain popular today. The great talent she received from God she gave back to him—by sharing it with others. Even as Europe was being torn apart by war, in drawing

Hummelwerkes Child Jesus

after drawing, Sister Innocentia captured the angelic faces of children filled with wonder and innocence. She died of tuberculosis at the early age of thirty-seven.

Some of Sister Hummel's drawings came to the notice of Franz Goebel, who arranged with the sisters to make three dimensional figurines from them. His company began to produce figurines based on her drawings in 1935. Priced at about one dollar, they came to America with returning soldiers from World War II. Now, depending on their rarity, some of these are valued in the thousands of dollars.

Hummelwerkes Child Jesus

VIII

Dressing Baby Jesus

Worldwide Customs

All manner of pious customs and other expressions of popular devotion can be found in the way people honor the images of Our Lord in his infancy.

Dressing the Infant

In a centuries-old tradition, many of the statues of the Christ Child are clothed and are often given wigs of human hair. From elaborate jeweled garments to the simplest handmade items, these are presented with love and devotion to the Christ Child.

The Infant of Prague has one of the largest and most interesting wardrobes in the world. His extensive and expensive wardrobe consists of more than seventy outfits, many decorated with precious jewels, especially pearls and Bohemian garnets. His oldest outfit dates from about 1700. Many pieces in his wardrobe are gifts from royalty; one dress was hand embroidered and presented by the Empress Maria Teresa. As proof of the wide extent of his cult, clothing has been sent from America, the Philippines, Vietnam, Austria, Italy, and Brazil. One outfit sent from a convent of Carmelite nuns near Shanghai has Chinese symbols embroidered around the hem that form a prayer for the Chinese people.

Many of the images, even those without a "miraculous" reputation, have received touching gifts from even the humblest devotees. One lovely depiction of the Christ Child in an old church in Mexico City wears a handmade crocheted baby cap and booties, presented to him by a pious devotee.

In Mexico, each year families purchase new clothing for the family statue of the Infant Jesus that lies in the manger scene at Christmas. On February 2, the feast of the Purification of the Virgin, or Candlemas, the little statue is dressed in the new finery and taken to the parish church to be blessed by the priest. This marks the official end of the Christmas season. Returned home, the statue is seated in a small decorated chair where he remains for the rest of the year until time to be placed again in the manger. Often, the new clothes are reproductions of ecclesiastical garments, but sometimes the clothing also represents the costume of a favorite saint. In some parts of Mexico City, the infants are carried in small, decorated baskets on this feast. Candy is sometimes put in the basket as a present for the Christ Child.

Dressing the Infant

Making His Place

A popular custom in many cultures throughout the world is to set up a small home altar for the Holy Child. These range from a simple shelf to an elaborate miniature representation of a church.

Furnishing His Place

Rocking the figure of the Christ Child in a cradle was a custom popular in the 1300s, especially in Germany and Austria. Usually

Making his place

done at Christmas, the child was rocked while the congregation sang, and afterward the pious came forward to venerate the image in his cradle. The custom was outlawed by ecclesiastical authorities in the sixteenth century but remained a common practice in convents and private homes for centuries.

Although cradles are rarely seen today, small chairs, beds, or thrones can be found in some churches, convents, and private homes, especially in Spanish-speaking countries. These small decorated pieces of furniture are provided for the images of the Christ Child and also for the images of the Virgin as an infant. Maria Bambina, a famous Italian wax sculpture, sleeps in a golden, highly decorated cradle at her shrine in Milan. The replica of this image at St. Thomas Church in Huntington, Massachusetts, is housed in a lovely reliquary but also lies on an elaborate little bed. Some statues are made with movable joints so they may be dressed or placed in a different position.

Most often today, the figures in the churches are displayed

Furnishing his place

inside a glass or crystal reliquary or box. In recent years, new and artistic methods of display have been devised in many places. One of the most stunning displays is in the church dedicated to the Holy Bell Ringer in Filzmoos, Austria. It dominates the apse of the church from a golden aureola in a hanging glass shrine, the work of the artist Jakob Adlhart.

Singing to the Babe

As in most Carmelite convents, there are a number of images of the Holy Child at the Carmelite monastery of Santa Clara, California. A number of charming traditions at the convent center on the Christ Child. During Advent the sisters draw billets, each containing a theme. On her recollection day, each sister may choose among three or four small cribs for a "day with Little Jesus." Each sister writes a song according to the theme of her billet, setting it to any tune she prefers. After Midnight Mass on Christmas Eve, the Holy Child is serenaded with the sisters' songs.

One treasured image in this convent is a wax figure from Alençon, the birthplace of St. Thérèse, the Little Flower, which is

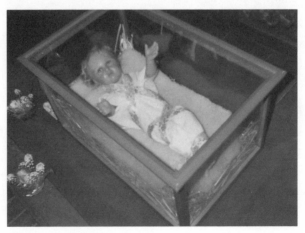

Singing to the Babe

kept in the Chapter room. The figure was given to the sisters over seventy-five years ago, just after World War I. Liturgical colors are used in the bands wrapped around the figure, which remains in a glass case for most of the year but is moved to a manger during the Christmas season.

Dancing for the Child

In the Philippines, part of the celebration of the Santo Niño of Cebu is a dance known as the *sinulog*. In a ritual of pre-Spanish origin, the dancers move two steps forward and one step backward to the rhythmic beat of drums. The movement somewhat resembles the current of the river and takes its name from the word *sulog,* meaning "the river's flow." As the dancer moves, he or she raises aloft an image of the Christ Child, a handkerchief, or a candle, and cries out "Pit Señor." Although it had pagan origins, the Augustinian missionaries appreciated native culture and preserved the dance to honor the Santo Niño.

In the Philippines today, the dancers accompany the *carrozza,* which bears the statue in procession through the streets of Cebu. A carnival-like atmosphere pervades this part of the religious cel-

Dancing for the Child

Raising the flag

Newspaper ads reporting favors from the Infant

ebration of the feast. In a number of cities in the United States where there is a large Filipino population, it has become popular to celebrate the feast of Santo Niño with the traditional procession and dances.

Raising the Flag

At the Shrine of the Infant Jesus in Viveknagar, India, a special flag is hoisted on Thursdays when the novena is prayed. The ceremony is witnessed by large numbers of people who pray for special intentions as the flag is raised, and then throw salt and flower petals at the flag.

At this same shrine, it is a popular custom to report favors from the infant by placing an ad in the local newspaper.

Food for the Feast

On January 6, the feast of the Epiphany, or during carnival in many countries, a special King's Cake is eaten. In some places, a tiny figure of a baby representing the Christ Child is hidden in the cake. In New Orleans, the guest who receives the slice of cake containing the figurine is obliged to be the host for the following year's Mardi Gras party.

Devotees of Colombia's Divino Niño consider it part of their devotion to give hot chocolate or other alms to the poor daily.

Gifts for Little Jesus

An entire book could easily be written about the variety of ex-votos and other votive offerings presented to the Christ Child throughout the world.

In Spanish-speaking countries, retablos, paintings on wood or tin, by folk artists are popular gifts presented in thanksgiving and usually show the story of the miracle. There are few words, but the pictures tell the story. The Niño de Atocha has so many ex-votos at his shrine in Fresnillo, Mexico, that a special building was constructed to hold them. In Mexico, a land of many churches, only the shrine of Our Lady of Guadalupe has more of these thanksgiving plaques. Other votive offerings to the Santo Niño

Food for the feast

Milagros given to Santo Niño de Atocha decorate a painting of St. Clare

are small metal Milagros. Formerly made of gold and silver, today's Milagros are more often made of base metal. These are made in a variety of shapes: hearts; body parts, such as arms and legs; animals, children, and adults in a praying pose. The nuns at the convent attached to the church have created an interesting form of art to display them. The Milagros are attached to paintings of the Virgin and the saints, covering all but the face and hands of the person portrayed. Today, photographs, hair, clothing, coins, and other forms of mementos are also found in abundance at this shrine.

Other shrines to the Holy Child have developed traditional particular votive gifts.

At Santo Niño de Atocha's shrine in New Mexico, it is traditional to present the Holy Child with baby shoes. Since he is said to travel about at night doing good works, he wears out his shoes, and they need to be replaced. Although they are not put on the image itself, his altar is always filled with tiny shoes.

The Child of Good Luck is given the little toys that all children love. Tiny cars and trucks, little china tea sets, and all manner of toys to delight a child can be found in front of his shrine in Coyacan, a suburb of Mexico City.

New clothes are a popular gift to the Child Jesus, Doctor of the Sick. One grateful client presented him with a little medical outfit, which included a tiny stethoscope and doctor's bag.

The traditional gift for one unnamed image in Mexico City is a stuffed animal. His glass-fronted shrine is so filled with these gifts of love and devotion that only the head of the statue can be seen.

I once put some china lambs on my home altar to the Christ Child. Through the years my children and family friends have added to his collection of small animals. Today, he has an impressive set of miniature animals from all parts of the world.

Everyone Loves a Parade

In Cuenca, Ecuador, there are a number of annual *pasadas,* or pageants, to honor the Christ Child from the first Sunday of Advent to the Epiphany. The largest of these is held on Christmas Eve and celebrates the Niño Viajero, or "traveling child." In 1961, a statue of the Christ Child was taken to Rome to be blessed by Pope John XXIII. On its return, someone in the watching crowd called out "Here comes the traveler!" The pageants recall the journey of Mary and Joseph to Bethlehem. In addition to the float carrying the Christ Child, there are other floats illustrating religious themes. Horses, llamas, and musicians join in to create a joyful and colorful event.

In Malta, a traditional procession with the Holy Child is held on Christmas Eve, carrying on a tradition begun by Blessed George Preca (1880–1962). Father Preca founded the Society of Christian Doctrine (MUSEUM) in 1907 for Catholic laymen and laywomen who wanted to dedicate themselves fully to God and to help the church in the faith formation of children, youth, and adults. The acronym MUSEUM stands for the Latin words *Magister Utinam Sequatur Evangelium Universus Mundus*— "Master, may the whole world follow the Gospel!" In 1921, Father Preca came up with the idea of making a procession with the Holy Child on Christmas Eve. He borrowed a large statue of the Christ Child to use for the procession, which took place in Hamrun, where he lived. The custom caught on and today these colorful processions are held in nearly all the cites and towns of Malta.

Everybody loves a parade

Rev. Msgr. George Preca

Wax statues of the Baby Jesus are found in many Maltese homes and are proudly displayed, especially during the Christmas season. Many of these were received as wedding gifts, a tradition throughout the Maltese Islands. Some of these, usually protected under glass domes and decorated with flowers, are antiques of Sicilian origin. Mass production of the little wax figures began in the post–World War I period. Since the early part of the twentieth century, the Society of Christian Doctrine produced thousands of the little bambinos, which were given as Christmas gifts to children who attended the various centers of the Society.

Pictures of Baby Jesus

Small devotional images of the Christ Child have been known and used for centuries in the form of icons, engravings, and woodcuts. Engraved in 1585–1586, a series of eighteen prints by Antoine Wierix (d. 1604) trace the conquest of the heart by the Infant Jesus. Early Jesuits carried small prints, many depicting the Child Jesus, on their mission ventures and used art in many ways to encourage devotion and teach the truths of the faith.

Many of the small devotional cards known as holy cards depict images of the Child Jesus. At first drawn or painted and decorated by individuals, they began to be mass-produced around the middle of the nineteenth century and hit a zenith in popularity around the middle of the twentieth century, when they were often presented as small awards in schools. Many charming and unique cards were handmade during Victorian times, using die-cut lace, pressed flowers, ribbons, and ornate calligraphy to decorate the printed images. The style changed and the cards lost popularity in the 1960s, but today they are enjoying a comeback and people have begun collecting these bits of religious ephemera again. Holy cards depicting the Child Jesus have been made in various countries throughout the world and are printed in many languages.

Today, in most of the Latin countries, small *estampitas* and larger lithographic prints of the various images of the Holy Child are still popular items.

Devotional image of Baby Jesus

Devotional image of Baby Jesus

*Devotional image of
Baby Jesus*

Stamping Jesus

In 2004, four wax images of the Christ Child, so popular in Malta and Gozo, were imprinted on a series of Christmas stamps issued by Maltapost. Mass production of these images of the Child Jesus began in the postwar period, and, during the twentieth century, the Society for Christian Doctrine produced thousands of them, which were given as Christmas gifts to the children who attended the Society's centers. The four images portrayed on the stamps are all in private collections; three are antique and one is modern. The 7c stamp features an antique papier mâché bambino from Italy. The 16c stamp shows a wax figure under a glass dome, decorated with flowers. This type of display is a popular custom in Malta.

Talking to the Christ Child

On Christmas day at the church of Santa Maria Aracoeli, the wooden statue of the Christ Child is moved to the main altar. The Roman children line up to recite a poem or to read a message to the Holy Bambino; they also sing happy songs. At Epiphany, the image is returned to his chapel.

Joyful Mysteries of the Rosary

Although all the mysteries of the rosary detail the life of Christ, the joyful mysteries are the ones that emphasize the Holy Child-hood. At the Annunciation, his coming Incarnation is announced. At the Visitation, John the Baptist is sanctified in his mother's womb and leaps for joy in anticipation of the savior. At the Nativity, Jesus enters the world in poverty as a weak human child and is heralded by the angels and adored by the Magi. At the

Presentation, although Jesus is not subject to the law of Moses he submits to it to teach obedience. Mary and Joseph are overjoyed at finding Jesus in the temple. Although he tells them he is "about his father's business," he returns with them to Nazareth and is obedient to them.

Prayers

A chaplet to the Infant Jesus, which is often erroneously attributed as an original part of the Prague devotion, came from the private revelations of Margaret Parigot at Beaune, France, and has spread worldwide. The chaplet has fifteen beads. It begins with a prayer of humble submission to God's will. On the first three beads, an Our Father is prayed in honor of the Holy Family. Twelve Hail Marys are prayed on the remaining beads in honor of the twelve years of Our Lord's childhood. The ejaculation "And the Word was made flesh and dwelt among us" is prayed before

Chaplet

each Our Father and the first Hail Mary. The chaplet closes with a request that the Holy Infant bless and protect us.

Four pious exercises in honor of the Holy Child have been enriched with indulgences: assisting at Midnight Mass on the feast of the nativity, assisting at Matins or Lauds on the same feast, taking part in a public novena before the feast, and making a novena before the twenty-fifth day of each month. A responsive prayer and two other individual prayers to the Holy Child are also indulgenced. However, there are hundreds of other approved prayers. Approved prayers accompany the devotion to each of the images mentioned in this book. In addition, novenas, scapulars, and chaplets enrich the popular devotion to many of them.

Thank You

This book would not have been possible without the generosity and help of friends throughout the world. Our sincere thanks for their assistance in this project to those listed below. If we have accidentally omitted anyone, we leave it to the Holy Child Jesus to carry our thanks and give them special blessings.

—*Ann Ball and Damian Hinojosa*

Mrs. Betsy Altenberger
Mr. Alfredo Amaya
Sr. Andrea, OCD
Sr. Carmella Ann, OCD
Basilica Pontificia de San Miguel, Madrid
Mr. Alejandro Bermudez
Rev. Alois Bilberauer, SVD
Mr. Eman Bonnici
Rev. John Boscoe, CSB
Sr. Clementia Burkard, SAC
Sr. Joan Calver, O.SS.R.
Carmelite Sisters of Cleveland, Ohio
Carmelite Sisters of Covington, Louisiana
Carmelite Sisters of Indianapolis
Sr. M. Carmelita Casso, IWBS
Catholic Action of Madrid, Spain
Sr. Madeline Cecile, LSJ
Renán "Cucuy" Almendárez Coello
Confraternity of Sto. Niño de Cebu of Houston
Mrs. Joan Cruz
Rev. Luis Diaz-Borunda

Mr. Al Ewer
Rev. James Farge, CSB
Rev. David Fernandez, SJ
Sr. Frossy Garcia
Sr. Carmen Maria Gonzalez, CVI
Rev. Mark Granito
Pbro. Gustavo Guijarro Montes
Rev. Leslaw Gwarek, SAC
Sr. Mary Pio Habermacker
Mr. Michael Heneghan
Mr. Stephen Ho
Holy Family Catholic Church, Missouri City, Texas
Instituto del Patrimonio Cultural of Caracas, Venezuela
Mrs. Susan Kerr
Ernest and Carmen Lopez
Kloister St. Maria Loreto
Mr. Joseph Kochiss
Ms. Anita Lewis
Mrs. Sandra Maola
Sr. Andrea Margarita
Sr. Helena Mayer, SHJ
Rev. William Hart McNichols
Sr. Marie Michelle, OCD
Rev. Teodoro Molino
Ms. Mary Mullins
Mrs. Karin Murthough
National Shrine of the Infant Jesus of Prague, Oklahoma
Mrs. Teri O'Toole
Sr. Dominic Ritter
Ms. Sue Rosebraugh
Sr. Rosa Sanchez, IWBS
Mr. Thomas Serafin
Rev. Kevin Shanley, OCarm

Rev. Al Sinasac, CSB
Sr. Connie Sonnen
Ms. Marcia Stein
Rev. David Thayer, SS
Mother Marie Therese OCD
Mother Agnes Therese, OCD
Rev. Vince Thompson, CSB
Rev. Maurice Vallence, SDB
Mr. Roy Vargese
Villa Lodovico
Dr. David Walker
Laurie Hollis-Walker
P. Joannes Zubiani, CP
Mr. and Mrs. Mark Zwick

In particular, we would like to thank the following for the use of their photographs:

Lic. Cruz Barceló Cedeño—Petare images
Gobernación del Estado Miranda—Petare images
Sr. Mary Jeanne Coderre, OCD—Carmelite images
Rev. Martin Kumar—India images
Mr. Jose Medina—Cuchilla images
Sr. Diane Meissurel,OCDS—Carmelite images
Teodoro de Molina—Gaucín images
Rev. Pablo Reartes—Argentine images
Rev. Anthony Timakus—Mexican images
Rev. Carl Tressler—Child of the Thorn images

Selected Bibliography

Albrecht, Barbara. *The Spiritual Legacy of Antonie Werr*. Munster-
schwarzach: Benedict Press, n.d.

Armour, Mary Andrew. *Cornelia*. Pompano Beach, Fla.: Exposi-
tion Press, 1984.

Ball, Ann. *Encyclopedia of Catholic Devotions and Practices*. Huntington, Ind.: Our Sunday Visitor, 2003.

———. *Holy Names of Jesus*. Huntington, Ind.: Our Sunday Visitor, 1990.

Bonaventure, Saint. *The Little Flowers of St. Francis*. New York:
E. P. Dutton, 1951.

Brankin, Patrick. *Bilingual Ritual of Hispanic Popular Catholicism*.
New Hope, Ky.: New Hope Publications, 2002.

Calver, Joan, OSSR. *In Memory of Me*. Liguori, Mo.: Monastery
of St. Alphonsus, 2004.

Christian, William A., Jr. *Apparitions in Late Medieval and Renaissance Spain*. Princeton, N.J.: Princeton University Press,
1981.

Christopher, Joseph, ed. *The Raccolta*. New York: Benzinger, 1943.

Clifton, James. *The Body of Christ: In the Art of Europe and New
Spain*. New York: Prestel, 1997.

Cruz, Joan. *Miraculous Images of Our Lord*. Rockford, Ill.: TAN
Books, 1993.

———. *Relics*. Huntington, Ind.: Our Sunday Visitor, 1984.

de la Cruz, Sor Juana Inés. *Obras Completas*. Mexico, D.F.:
Editorial Porrua, 1969.

Descouvemont, Pierre. *Therese and Lisieux*. Grand Rapids: Eerd-
mans, 1996.

Doheny, Wm. J., CSC. *The Life of Saint Birgitta of Sweden*.
Privately printed, 1980.

Escoto, Augusto Isunza. *Plateros y el Santo Niño de Atocha.* Fresnillo, Zacatecas: Calle de Plateros, 1980.

Eytel, Loa, trans. *The Hummel Book.* Stuttgart: Emil Fink-Verlag, 1968.

Fenik, Beernie, trans. *Das Kloster St. Andreas und Das Hilfreiche Sarner Jesuskind.* Sarnen: Benedictine Nuns, 1982.

Fernandez Rodriguez, O.P. Pedro. *Biografia de la Madre Maria Angelica Alvarez Icaza.* Salamanca: Editorial San Sebastián, 1993.

Filzmoos. Salzburg: Verlag St. Peter, n.d.

Hamburger, Jeffrey. *The Visual and the Visionary: Art and Female Spirituality in Late Medieval Germany.* New York: Zone Books, 1998.

Hebert, Albert J., SM. *Mary, Why Do You Cry?* Paulina, La.: Albert J. Hebert, 1985.

Heneghan, Michael. *Devotion to the Divine Child Jesus.* Galway: St. Macartan Books, 2003.

Hutin, Magdeleine. *Jesus Love.* Little Sisters of Jesus, 1945.

Kerr, Susan Anderson. "The Holy Child of Atocha: The History and Meaning of a Catholic Devotion." Unpublished paper. Austin, 2004.

Klapisch-Zuber, Christiane. *Women, Family, and Ritual in Renaissance Italy.* Chicago: University of Chicago Press, 1985.

Lopez de Lara, J. Jesus. *El Niño de Santa Maria de Atocha.* Fresnillo, Zacatecas: Santuario de Plateros, 1980.

Lord, Bob, and Penny Lord. *Miracles of the Child Jesus.* Morrilton, Ariz.: Journeys of Faith, 2002.

Love Can Do All: The History of the Carmel of Buffalo. Buffalo, N.Y.: Carmel of Buffalo, 1995.

Lozano, John. *Jeanne Chezard de Matel and the Sisters of the Incarnate Word.* Chicago: Claret Center, 1983.

Martinez, Jose Lopez. *El Santo Niño de Atocha.* Fresnillo, Zacatecas: Santuario de Plateros, n.d.

McDonagh, Kathleen, trans. *Jeanne Chezard de Matel Complete Works,* vol. 6, *Treatises.* Corpus Christi: IWBS Archives, 2004.

Menendez, Josefa. *The Way of Divine Love.* Westminster: Newman Press, 1961.

Mujica, Barbara. *Antología de la literatura española: Edad Media.* New York: John Wiley & Sons, 1991.

———. *Antología de la literatura española: Renacimiento y Siglo de Oro.* New York: John Wiley & Sons, 1991.

The New Oxford Annotated Bible with the Apocrypha: Revised Standard Version. New York: Oxford University Press, 1973.

Novena Biblica al Divino Niño Jesús. Bogota: Apostolado Biblica Catolico, 2003.

Novena Y Tridua al Milagrosisimo Niño de Atocha. Guadalajara: Gregorio Davila, n.d.

Nolan, Brian J. "The Religious Name of St. Therese." In *Carmel in the World,* vol. 42, no. 2. Rome: Institutum Carmelitanum, 2003.

Onasch, Konrad, and Annemarie Schnieper. *Icons,* trans. by Daniel Conklin. New York: Riverside Book Company, 1995.

Padre Pío of Pietrelcina. *Letters,* vol. 1, *San Giovanni Rotondo.* Edizioni Padre Pío da Pietrelcina, 1984.

Pescador, Juan Javier. "Seeking the Holy Child of the Border: The Historical Origins of the Santo Niño de Atocha, 1704–1848." Unpublished paper.

Ponce, Manuel. *Holy Infant of Good Health.* Morelia, Mexico: Shrine, 1961.

Rodriguez, Pedro, OP. *Biografia de la Madre Ma. Angélica Alvarez Icaza.* Salamanca: Editorial San Esteban, 1993.

Rothemund, B. *Gnadenreiche Jesulein.* Autenried: Buch-Kunstverlag-Autenried, 1982.

Il S. Bambino di Aracoeli. Rome: Convento Aracoeli, 1979.

El Santuario de Chimayo. Santa Fe: Spanish Colonial Arts Society, 1956.

Stevens, Barbara. "Cebu City's Resplendent Christ Child." *Our Sunday Visitor* (Huntington, Ind.). October 25, 1992, p. 5.

Suarez, Restituto, OSA. *Perpetual Novena to Santo Niño de Cebu.* Cebu City: Augustinian Fathers, 1960.

Teresa de Jesús. *Obras Completas.* Madrid: M. Aguilar, 1950.

Therese, Marie, SMCJ. *Cornelia Connelly.* Westminster, Md.: Neumann Press, 1963.

Toal, M. F., trans. *The Sunday Sermons of the Great Fathers,* vol. 1. Swedesboro, N.J.: Preservation Press, 1996.

Uhlorn, Cecile. "At Home in Sarnen, Switzerland." *Canticle* (Spring 2002): 1.

Valle, Ana. "Conozca el NiñoPa, consentido de Xochimilco." *Simi Informer* (Mexico, D.F.). January 24, 2005, p. 12.

Varghese, Roy. *God Fleshed.* New York: Crossroad, 2001.

———. *God Sent.* New York: Crossroad, 2000.

Weiser, Francis X. *Handbook of Christian Feasts and Customs.* New York: Harcourt Brace and World, 1958.

Zollner, Frank, *Leonardo da Vinci.* Cologne: Taschen, 2000.

Index